DROPSHIPPING

THE ULTIMATE STEP BY STEP GUIDE TO BUILD YOUR E-COMMERCE BUSINESS AND START MAKING MONEY ONLINE.
CREATE YOUR PASSIVE INCOME IN 60 DAYS.

LOGAN STORE

© Copyright 2019 by Logan Store
All rights reserved.

The content contained within this book may not be reproduced, duplicated or transmitted without direct written permission from the author or the publisher.

Under no circumstances will any blame or legal responsibility be held against the publisher, or author, for any damages, reparation, or monetary loss due to the information contained within this book. Either directly or indirectly.

<u>Legal Notice:</u>

This book is copyright protected. This book is only for personal use. You cannot amend, distribute, sell, use, quote or paraphrase any part, or the content within this book, without the consent of the author or publisher.

Disclaimer Notice:

Please note the information contained within this document is for educational and entertainment purposes only. All effort has been executed to present accurate, up to date and reliable, complete information. No warranties of any kind are declared or implied. Readers acknowledge that the author is not engaging in the rendering of legal, financial, medical or professional advice. The content within this book has been derived from various sources. Please consult a licensed professional before attempting any techniques outlined in this book.

By reading this document, the reader agrees that under no circumstances is the author responsible for any losses, direct or indirect, which are incurred as a result of the use of information contained within this document, including, but not limited to, — errors, omissions, or inaccuracies.

Table of Contents

INTRODUCTION 8

CHAPTER 1: ENTREPRENEURSHIP MADE EASY WITH DROPSHIPPING 11

    THE WINNING MINDSET NEEDED 12
    WELCOME TO THE WORLD OF DROPSHIPPING 17
    METHOD #1 - DROPSHIPPING DIRECTLY FROM SUPPLIERS 21
    METHOD #2 - DROPSHIPPING VIA ONLINE RETAILERS 25
    METHOD #3 - DROPSHIPPING VIA AMAZON FBA 28
    WHO BENEFITS THE MOST FROM THIS TYPE OF BUSINESS? 32

CHAPTER 2: THE GOOD, BAD AND EVERYTHING ELSE YOU NEED TO KNOW 35

    THE BENEFITS OF DROPSHIPPING 36
    DROPSHIPPING DRAWBACKS 39
    HOW TO GET STARTED WITH YOUR DROPSHIPPING BUSINESS 45
    WHAT'S MY PRODUCT? 50
    WHAT'S MY NICHE? 51
    WHAT PRODUCTS SHOULD I NOT SELL? 53
    WHAT'S MY PAYMENT GATEWAY? 55
    AM I TRUSTWORTHY? 57

CHAPTER 3: THE FIRST FEW STEPS 58

Dropshipping Platforms 58
- *Amazon FBA* *59*
- *Yahoo Store* *61*
- *Shopify* *62*
- *Oberlo* *63*
- *WooCommerce* *64*
- *BigCommerce* *64*
- *Magento* *65*
- *OpenCart* *66*

Other Dropshipping Related Sites That Prove Useful 68
Dropshipping Websites for Sale 70
How to Find the Best Niches 72
How to Find Your Suppliers 77
Dropshipping Suppliers to Stay Away From 81

CHAPTER 4: GET CLICKING AND START BUILDING 83

Is A Dropshipping Website Necessary? 83
Creating a Website for Your Online Business 86
Why Choose BlueHost? 90
How Do I Know If My Dropshipping Website Is Any Good? ... 91
How to Scale Your Business 93
- *Strategy #1- Building Trust* *96*
- *Strategy #2- Creating an Amazing Offer* *96*
- *Strategy #3- Preparing to Pivot* *97*
- *Strategy #4- Choosing ePacket* *98*
- *Strategy #5- Importing the First 25 Items* *98*
- *Strategy #6- Encouraging Upsell and Cross-sell Marketing* ... *99*
- *Strategy #7 - Market on Social Media* *100*

Running Your Business 100

CHOOSING YOUR DROPSHIPPING BUSINESS STRUCTURE 103
DEALING WITH SALES TAX AND LOCAL LICENSES 106

CHAPTER 5: HANDLING YOUR AFFAIRS 108

HOW TO HANDLE CUSTOMER CARE 108
HANDLING ORDER DELAYS 109
HANDLING OUT OF STOCK PRODUCTS 110
EVERY LITTLE BIT HELPS 111
HOW TO DEAL WITH FRAUDS 113
HOW TO HANDLE PRODUCT RETURNS 118
SHOULD I OFFER PRODUCT RETURNS AND WHY? 124
OTHER CONSIDERATIONS TO KEEP IN MIND 128

CHAPTER 6: SUCCESS IS ALMOST YOURS 131

ORDER FULFILLMENT - WHAT IS IT ANYWAY? 131
CREATING A POSITIVE SALES EXPERIENCE FOR YOUR CUSTOMER 135
WHAT TO DO WHEN YOU CAN'T FULFIL YOUR ORDERS 138
TIPS FOR SUCCESS 139
DROPSHIPPING MISTAKES TO AVOID 143
BONUS TIPS TO KEEP A GOOD RELATIONSHIP GOING WITH YOUR SUPPLIER .. 152

CONCLUSION 154

Introduction

Every day brings with it the possibility of something new and exciting. That's one of the best things about running a business of your own. Two days are never going to be the same and if you're someone who thrives on this kind of excitement, then entrepreneurship could be your calling. Making the decision to become your own boss and take control of your destiny is only the beginning. What's an even bigger decision is to choose *what* type of business model is going to be right for you.

If you're an entrepreneur who's just starting out, here are some of the traits you might be searching for in a potential business model:

- Something that is low risk.
- A business model that doesn't necessarily require a lot of initial capital to invest in.
- A business model that you can run online from anywhere you may be, because all you need is a laptop and a good internet connection.
- Something that is easy to set-up.
- Something easy to implement without an unreasonably high overhead cost to contend with.

Did you find yourself nodding yes to these statements? Then the kind of business model that you're looking for is known as *dropshipping*.

The beauty of dropshipping is that you don't need to keep actual stock or inventory of the items you want to sell. Dropshipping, as you will quickly discover, is one of the easiest businesses in the e-commerce world that you could start with. It is low-risk and low-investment which is great for novices starting their own business. It does not involve much monetary gamble, the way a traditional brick and mortar business would. You don't have to deal with the cost of the rental, utilities, renovation, employee salaries, licensing and permits for the location that you've based it. All of that is now unnecessary and those are just some of the many reasons why dropshipping businesses have skyrocketed over the years, as more and more entrepreneurs are taking the plunge and starting something of their own.

Business can be daunting for any first-timer, as well as a seasoned entrepreneur. There's always a risk of making one wrong decision that could end up jeopardizing the entire business. The uncertainty of whether your business is going to make it, the high risk involved, the pressure of trying to get your business off the ground and how to gain market traction is a lot for anyone to handle, especially if they haven't got much business experience to begin with. That's why dropshipping offers the perfect solution. You get to ease into the business world without the high stakes risk while you test the market and understand how to sell online, what drives traffic, how to turn that traffic into sales and what it takes to optimize sales. If you were looking for a business model that was going to be the perfect learning curve while still bringing in some profit on a regular basis, you've found it.

With so many books about the subject in the market, we greatly appreciate you choosing this book! Please know that all efforts are made to ensure all information is useful for you!

Chapter 1: Entrepreneurship Made Easy with Dropshipping

It's so easy these days starting a new business in the digital space. Technology has certainly brought about many benefits that have no doubt enriched and empowered our lives in many ways. One such benefit is the ability to start a new business online. Behind all those new small, medium and micro businesses, that you see online there is an entrepreneur and owner of that business who is working hard and doing their best every day to achieve success.

It's admirable, what they're doing. It takes guts, determination, willpower and a combination of several other factors to build a successful business from the ground up. To take that leap of faith and follow your passion is a decision that not just anyone can make. It takes an individual with the winning mindset to chase their entrepreneurial dreams, even with a seemingly easy enough business like dropshipping.

The Winning Mindset Needed

While a successful business is a combination of blood, sweat, tears and a whole host of other factors that have come together to contribute towards its achievement, there is one other, essential element that every entrepreneur needs to have on their side. You've probably heard it being mentioned often enough but never given much thought to it. All that is about to change though, since it is now more important than ever that this vital ingredient exists in the forefront of your mind. Without it, you'll find yourself struggling every step of the way on your rise to the top, no matter how prepared or well thought out your business plan may be. What you need is known as the *winning mindset.*

The winning mindset is the game-changer, the key to turn your vision into reality. The ongoing state of mind that is needed to fuel your motivation and desire to keep pushing forward, no matter what obstacles are thrown your way. The mindset that is going to fill you with the positive enthusiasm, you need to believe you can do this, to never give up until you've accomplished what you set out to do. Every successful individual out there who has achieved something great and made a name for themselves started building their success from within, in their mind. They visualized it and believed in that vision so much that they started to conceive it, make it their reality.

Mind over matter. What the mind can conceive, it can achieve. It's all in your mind. These wise old sayings are still as relevant today as when they first came about because they perfectly sum out what an important role our mind plays. How *powerful* our thoughts can be if we learn how to channel it properly. An idea, when nurtured, can initiate a chain reaction of events that bring that idea to fruition. A simple idea can build a business empire so successful it can last through the generations. When you have a winning mindset, you believe anything is possible and that belief is the most powerful force you can have on your side when you're beginning one of the most challenging tasks you will ever take on in your life. Building a new business.

For every one person who has achieved success, there are 9 others who failed, even though they may have had the same dreams. Those many who fail to make their dreams come true, is because they didn't have the right mindset needed to drive them to action. Without the winning mindset, they're not *convinced* that they can do this and that's the difference between them and those who have gone on to pursue their passions. With the right mindset, you can move mountains and you only need to read the memoirs and success story of those who have already gone the distance. The odds that they had to overcome were not easy, but they *believed* that they could do it, *believed* that they could win and that's what they did.

Before beginning your dropshipping business, let's take a moment to assess your mindset. Where is it at right now? Do you believe you're a winner? Or are you still harboring some doubts about whether you're making the right decision? To build a successful dropshipping business, there's only room for the former and if you're not quite there yet, it's time to prep your mind and starts building the foundation of the winning mindset with the following pillars needed for success:

- **A Strong Desire** - Your desire for success must be so strong that it's all you can think about from the moment you wake up in the morning, until you go to bed at night. What is it that you desire most? Let your answers be your driving force.

- **Unwavering Focus** - There are going to be a lot of distractions along the way, challenges that will push you beyond your comfort zone and test your willpower. The only thing that's going to get you through it all is an unwavering focus on what your end goals are.

- **Setting Clear Intentions** - Having clear intentions is the same as setting goals for yourself. Be clear about why you're doing this from the beginning. Are you starting your dropshipping business for fun? Or do you have much bigger plans for it in mind? Clear intentions, along with goals, will help you with a lot of the decisions you're going to have to make as a business owner.

- **Set Goals** - Whenever anyone asks why you've started a dropshipping business, you should be able to explain your reason why without hesitation. You've got your intention and you've got your goals, which are the directions you need, to help you navigate the map towards success. Goals help you measure how much progress you're making and more importantly, whether you're progressing in the right direction, the way that you should be. Your goals give you a sense of purpose, something to work towards and each time you find yourself just one step closer, your belief in yourself strengthens with every victory. That's a winner.

- **Being Patient** - Part of being a winner is knowing that good things take time. A business is not something that is going to instantly turn a profit overnight. Yes, it has the potential to make a lot of money and help you achieve your financial goals, but it takes time. Sometimes a lot of time. Having the patience to wait for the delayed gratification is how you set yourself apart from the others who eventually gave up because they couldn't wait any longer.

- **Commitment** - You've done all that you can to give your business its best chance for success, but without the commitment needed to stick to your action plan, it's not going to work. A winning mindset must be accompanied with the commitment needed to consistently take action, even if you don't see instantaneous results happening before your very eyes. Something is happening and you might not always be able to see it, but every action taken has a consequence. The commitment to consistent action is how you achieve long-term results.

The Winning Mindset

Picture 1

Welcome to the World of Dropshipping

Dropshipping is a term you would no doubt have heard or be familiar with if you've been scouring the e-commerce world, exploring the available options and business models. Comparatively, one of the easier business models to establish, dropshipping is ideal for the entrepreneur who wants to get into the business game but might not have a lot of capital to invest or business experience either.

Dropshipping is business which is focused on order fulfillment, just like any other business would be. The difference between this and your regular business models is that with dropshipping, the owner does not keep any of the physical products ready stocked with them. That's right; you're selling products, without owning any of the products. When a customer places an order, that order is sent to a third-party supplier that you're working closely with. The supplier is the one who will be responsible for shipping your order to your customer.

Here's what a normal business cycle might look like without the presence of dropshipping:

- You purchase products from the supplier so your business always has inventory on hand.
- These products are stored by your business as you wait

- patiently for a customer to come along and make a purchase.
- When they do, you package the products and handle the shipping yourself.

Now, with the dropshipping process, on the other hand, this is what the business cycle might look like:

- You source the suppliers you want to work with.
- You list the products for sale on your site and wait until a customer makes an order.
- Once an order is placed, you pass those details along to your supplier.
- The supplier then packages the goods ordered and ships them directly to the customer's doorstep.

There's one thing that needs to be clear before you begin, though. Dropshipping is easy enough to understand, but it's not a business model that is going to get you rich quick. In theory, it sounds like running this type of business should be much easier than the traditional brick and mortar types, but make no mistake; dropshipping still comes with its own cons and challenges that need to be contended with. At the end of the day, it is still a business and like every other business, it's going to take hard work and commitment to get it off the ground and running successfully. This is going to be something you must be prepared to do from the very beginning.

For the entrepreneur who's just starting out for the first time, dropshipping is the perfect business model, to begin with. Since you're not physically holding onto the inventory yourself, you're free to sell as many products as you can manage on your site, provided you have the reliable suppliers to help you fulfill your orders. Sell as many, or as little, as you'd like, although of course, the more you sell the more money you potentially stand to gain. Another reason why beginners will love this model is the low up-front capital that is needed to begin. Since you do not have to purchase any of the physical inventory yourself, you don't have to fork out large sums purchasing products when the suppliers will be storing them for you.

The dropshipping business is made up of three main players:

- **The Manufacturers -** The party who is responsible for the creation of the product you're selling. Since manufacturers don't sell their products directly to the public, they rely on businesses like your dropshipping model to do it for them. There's a good chance you'll be able to negotiate the cheapest prices when you buy and work directly with them. However, most manufacturers will have a minimum requirement that you'll need to purchase and depending on that amount; you sometimes might need to sort out the storage options yourself.

- **The Wholesalers** – It is the group that makes purchases directly from the manufacturers and they do it in bulk to meet the minimum purchase quota. If your dropshipping business is serving a selected niche, wholesalers are a good option to consider working with.

- **The Vendors** - That's you. The one with the dropshipping business. You're the vendor and your role in the dropshipping dynamic is to sell these products directly to the customers at a slightly more marked up price.

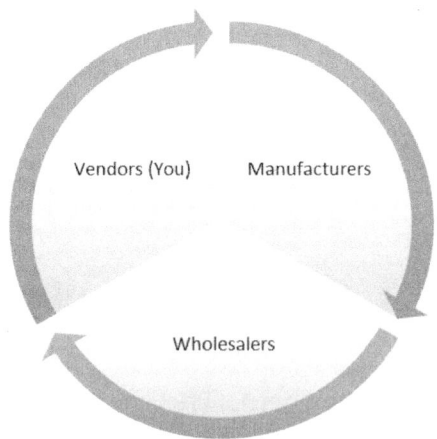

The 3 Main Players in Dropshipping
Picture 2

There are also three different types of dropshipping methods for you to choose from. Prior to this, dropshipping primarily consisted of a service where suppliers would ship their products directly to the customer if they had the logistical means to do so. Naturally, since technology and the offerings of the online world evolve and change so rapidly, dropshipping wasn't left behind. Today, this service has grown beyond just the classic dropshipping method, with many sellers today even utilizing Amazon's fulfilled by Amazon (FBA) service to get Amazon to do the dropshipping for them. Let's break down the three dropshipping methods which are heavily used today:

Method #1 - Dropshipping Directly from Suppliers

The classic method is still as good as new. When dropshipping directly from the suppliers, you, as the vendor, will need to work on establishing a good, professional working relationship with the suppliers you choose to retain as part of your business. There's going o be a lot of negotiation involved here until both parties can come to terms of the agreement that benefit both. Once you've locked down the suppliers you're happy to work with, you'll then move to list their products on your web stores.

With this approach, there's very little chance that you're ever going to see, own or touch the products that you're selling. You're purely the middleman in this scenario and the major advantage of this method is the value creation. You're establishing a genuine relationship with a supplier that you know, as opposed to working with dropshipping platform giants like Aliexpress or Amazon and these genuine relationships formed can help add quite a substantial value to the business world. When you're working with a supplier in China for example, who may have the products but not necessarily the skills, knowledge or resources needed to market it to the rest of the world, that's where you come in with the expertise they need and create real value for their products. Producing a creative, professional description for each product, listing and promoting them in an appealing way that customers can relate to, along with the top-notch customer service element, bridges the gap and makes online shopping a global experience.

Another advantage to this method is you get to choose the supplier you want to work with and it is up to you to choose a partner who is going to care just as much about your mutual business interests as you do. As the middleman, you must be comfortable surrendering control over your products to the supplier and if you don't get someone with the same mutual interests to make this arrangement work, that's going to cause some major problems that could potentially affect your business.

For example, if you cared about shipping out quickly and on time but the supplier didn't, the customer will see it as you failing to deliver on your timely shipping promise. On the other hand, if you worked with a supplier who was professional and just as committed to providing a great business experience the way you were, constantly communicating and updating on the status of the shipment or what's happening in general with stock and inventory, that makes for a beautiful working relationship that could go a long way. Having a personal relationship with your supplier can make a big difference to your business.

Of course, there are disadvantages to this method too; one of them being that sourcing these suppliers to work with can be somewhat difficult. Since finding a supplier is one of the most critical factors needed for the success of your business, it's crucial to find one that you can see yourself having a long-term working relationship with. This endeavor, however, could take weeks or even months of constant searching and hard work before you find the perfect fit for your business. You want a supplier who's not only professional but communicates effectively and, more importantly, is a business partner you can trust. This process can't be rushed, so you must be patient and prepared for the fact that it is going to take time.

Since you're going to have to rely heavily on communication, which poses yet another potential problem for human error to occur. When miscommunication happens, it's going to affect your business and possibly your clients too depending on what happens. If your supplier fails to update you on the availability of the stock, it's going to affect your ability to fulfill the orders, which is going to leave you with some very unhappy clients who might take their business elsewhere if they were counting on your shipment. In any kind of business, reputation is everything and when you're a startup, it is very risky to deal with anything that could risk jeopardizing your reputation right from the start. Order cancellations reflect negatively on your business, even if it is not entirely your fault and negative reviews from customers are hard to bounce back from. True, instances like these are rare, but they do happen every now and again, which brings us back to why it is so important to find a supplier that you can work professionally with.

Then there's the fact that relationships, any kind of relationship, needs to be nurtured and attended to. Trust takes time and a lot of effort invested in effective communication. Nurturing relationships right from the ground up is just as time-consuming as starting a business from scratch, but if you do it right, it'll be worth it.

Method #2 - Dropshipping via Online Retailers

Online retailers like Amazon, AliExpress, eBay and Shopify, for example, are some major names in the dropshipping business that have established quite a steady reputation for themselves online. Mention Amazon and customers immediately get the impression that products are more reliable and value for money because of the reputation associated with Amazon. This is an arbitrage model of dropshipping, where you as the vendor will scout for arbitrage prices between two or more of these retailers and advantage on the price difference to make a profit. Check out the example we have here for you. Let's say you found an item that you liked on Amazon for $20 and you found the exact same item on Shopify for $30. You will then be able to leverage this difference to your advantage by ordering the item from Amazon for the $20 price but selling it on Shopify for the $30 price tag. Your profit then would be $10. Instead of having a real relationship with a supplier, what you're doing instead is buying products from one online retailer and selling it for a slightly higher price on another platform. Profits are small, but it's still a profit if you don't mind the margins.

One benefit of this approach is you eliminate the time and effort needed to build a relationship with a supplier since you're making your profits through the arbitrage pricing difference between different online retailers. Another advantage is that you have options for multiple suppliers when it comes to sourcing your products. Most dropshipping platforms sell the same kind of products, which means that you minimize the risk involved with running out of stock. When one supplier doesn't have what you need, you can always go to another.

The available automation tools with this method also make life much easier for you, taking away the bulk of your manual labor so you can focus instead on another important aspect for a successful business. Your customer service. ProfitSraper, PriceYak, Yaballe, Salefreaks and DsmTool are just some of the many dropshipping arbitrage solutions that will automatically look and scan for the best prices around, which means you don't have to manually do it yourself. These platforms also list these products automatically, so you don't have to and they even re-price your items if the prices on the source platforms get updated.

The downside with this method, though, is that it isn't sustainable for a long-term business. Competition is high in dropshipping and all it takes is one bad review or poor customer service to drive you out of business. A quick search online is all it takes to see how high the competition is and when a customer isn't happy, they're not likely to return when there are several other vendors offering the same products that you are. Since profit margins are very small with this dropshipping method, you should cover any customer returns and the cost of shipping returns may be higher than your profit margin, which then defeats the purpose.

There is also the absence of value creation with this approach. When you're selling an item that is easily available on several other prices for slightly higher or lower prices, you're not adding any value to it. A profitable business can only be built when you create something of value that your customers need and want. Plus, a customer might be discouraged from buying from you ever again if they ordered an item from you through Shopify only to receive it in an Amazon package. They might just choose to buy directly from Amazon in the future instead of going through your site to do it and that's a potential loss of business right there.

Small profit margins are another drawback when you rely just on arbitrage pricing alone to run your business. With the available automation solutions that keep popping up, margins are getting smaller and the competition stiffer. Imagine going up against vendors who are automatically listing thousands of items, doing the exact same thing that you are. This just further decreases your odds of making a profit, unless you've got repeat customers who love your service enough to keep coming back to you. To make a sizeable profit, you need to maintain a consistently large sales volume which is almost impossible without building genuine relationships with the suppliers themselves.

Method #3 - Dropshipping via Amazon FBA

Launched in 2006, Amazon's FBA has been a hit with many vendors who now use this to conduct their dropshipping business. Using this approach, you would buy your items in bulk from the supplier and then ship it to any one of the many warehouses Amazon has. Amazon will then store the inventory for you and when an order comes, it ships out the item on your behalf directly to the customer. One advantage with this method is that you'll be able to use Amazon's FBA service to fulfill your orders that come in from other sales avenues too. You could, for instance, process orders that come in from Walmart of eBay and fulfill them from your existing Amazon FBA account.

However, because you do need to buy and store the items in Amazon's warehouses, this isn't a 100% percent dropshipping model. To truly benefit from this method, you need to be a seller who has enough traction and necessary experience needed to be able to predict the demand for your orders so you're not stuck with inventory that never gets sold. Amazon's FBA services are still a good option to consider though because you're essentially utilizing the services of one of the top logistics operators in the world. You and your customers can have peace of mind knowing that any orders placed through Amazon are going to be processed quickly and delivered as soon as possible.

Listing your products on Amazon also comes with extra perks, such as being eligible for their Super Saver Shipping, Buy Box and Amazon Prime shipping options which are more than likely to lead to greater customer conversion rates. Plus, Amazon will handle any customer returns for you, so you don't have to worry about that aspect. If you were to compare the profit margins made with buying items in bulk from wholesalers and individually dropshipping products from suppliers only when the orders come in from customers, profit margins with the Amazon FBA approach are much better, since you've already bought the item at a bulk price.

The disadvantage with this method, however, is that Amazon's FBA fees could end up eating into your profit margins more than you would like. You're also going to have to fork out money for the storage, which is again going to eat into your profit margins as opposed to the classic dropshipping approach where you don't have to pay to purchase stock in advance.

Another drawback that not a lot of vendors might like is that Amazon's warehouse is home to tens of thousands of products from other vendors. They store everything together per item type, which means that your product is going to be mixed in with all the other products stored by different vendors. The slight risk with this one is because everything is lumped in together, there's a chance that the product which gets sent to the customer is not the exact same product you initially sent to Amazon. A slight risk, but still a risk nonetheless.

Once you've determined the kind of products you would like to sell on your site, you can begin sourcing for the suppliers needed. Since you're not holding onto any physical stock yourself, the images of the products you're going to be selling are coming directly from your supplier. Essentially, you as the owner of a dropshipping business are like the middleman. You're the link between the customer and the supplier. When the customer needs something, they go to your website, make a purchase and you pass the details onto the supplier for them to handle the shipping. The customer never knows the supplier and the supplier never knows the customer. The two won't directly be dealing with each other. They'll be dealing with you instead. You're going to be the face, the representative of both parties and that is why your dropshipping business exists.

The products that you list on your site are usually already paid for. Dropshipping vendors generally pay for the items but at a discounted rate since they work directly with the suppliers, wholesalers or manufacturers. The profit margin is going to come from the difference between what you had to pay the supplier and the price that the customer paid for it. Your job in this situation is to stay on top of your inventory and constantly keeping tabs on the numbers so you minimize the risk of listing items which are no longer in stock.

This arrangement works out well since you only pay the suppliers for their products *after* you have received payment from the customer. This is fantastic in fact since it eliminates the risk of having outdated or unsold inventory on your hands, which is something that brick and mortars must deal with all the time.

As a dropshipping vendor, your efforts are going to be focused solely on marketing and promoting your website and your products, since you don't have to focus on managing your inventory. Therefore, managing your online presence and maintaining good customer service is going to be the primary aspects that your dropshipping business should be focusing most of its efforts on.

A dropshipping business is easy enough that it can be managed on the side without having to quit your full-time job. If you're not ready to lose the security of a steady income just yet but still want to try your hand at running your own business, this is the model for you. If you're looking for a business that is going to give you a large profit margin though, then dropshipping might not be it, since your earnings are going to be small after paying your suppliers. Not to mention the cost of running your website, although admittedly, these are still much smaller costs incurred compared to running any other type of business model.

On its own, you can rest assured that dropshipping is a business model that is perfectly legal. Depending on which supplier you're working with, that's when you may or may not encounter some legal issues. To be on the safe side, it's best to have a contract or [Dropshipping Agreement](#) drawn up just to protect yourself.

Who Benefits the Most from This Type of Business?

Those who are new to the e-commerce world have the most to gain by venturing into the dropshipping business. However, if you're doing just dropshipping alone and hoping to get a roaring business going, you might be disappointed to find that it's not going to be that easy. Dropshipping can complement an existing e-commerce store or vendor who is already well established, but starting a profitable business from scratch is going to be a long process which, given the small profit margins, might not happen.

Looking at the pros and cons of dropshipping, the entrepreneurs who have the most to gain from this model include:

- New entrepreneurs who have no prior business experience and are looking for something to learn.
- Entrepreneurs with very small capital to start and those looking for a low-risk business model.
- Entrepreneurs who are looking to test the waters and see if there's potential before they decide to jump in with larger investments.
- Entrepreneurs who are not keen on holding onto large inventory stocks that run the risk of not being sold.
- The entrepreneur who is looking for the least expensive business model to get their start in.

Dropshipping is not going to be the best idea if you:

- Are concerned about only achieving high-profit margins.
- Don't have the time to invest in marketing.
- Are not comfortable about having little to no control over the running of your business operations.
- Are looking to build a brand image for your business, something your customers will immediately associate you with. Like Nike for example. Think Nike and you immediately think of sports performance related merchandise and equipment.

- Are not going to be happy or satisfied with small profit margins, which is one of the biggest drawbacks to the dropshipping model. If you're looking to make anywhere from 50% to 100% profit per item, you might be better off looking for another type of business model.

Chapter 2: The Good, Bad and Everything Else You Need to Know

Becoming an e-commerce entrepreneur can be an exciting venture. As challenging as running a business can be, it's also a very exciting prospect for those who love the ups, the downs and the unpredictability that only the business world can provide. It's nothing like having a steady 9-5 job where every day is just as predictable as the day before. Being an entrepreneur is something else altogether.

Dropshipping may be one of the easier business models to start with, but like every other business; you still have to work hard to build your business into something substantial. If you've always wanted to see whether you've got what it takes to make it as a business person, this is the place to test what you're made of. Whether you've got the time, energy, commitment and patience that is needed to build this small-scale business from scratch and one day, launch a much bigger business undertaking of your own.

The Benefits of Dropshipping

Now that you've familiarized yourself with the basics of the dropshipping business model, let's take a closer look at the benefits that you can expect with this approach and why dropshipping could be a good idea for you:

- **It's Extremely Easy to Set Up** - If you're looking for an easy business that requires as minimal work as possible in the set-up part, this is it. To begin your dropshipping business, all you'll need is a good website, reliable suppliers and products to sell. That's it! No renovation, no rental agreements to deal with, no scouring for good locations to set up your business, none of that hassle to deal with.

- **No Capital Needed** - Even if you're on a shoestring budget or without a dime to your name, you can still launch a dropshipping business. You can still get suppliers on your team without a cent since you only need to pay them a portion of what you make from your sale, *once the customer has paid you.*

- **The Low Cost of Overhead** - This is a major plus point for entrepreneurs who don't have a lot of capital to work with and are not keen on taking out a business loan because that's far too risky (what if the business fails?). Without the need to purchase any inventory upfront, you need very little investment on your part to get started. Even on less than $100 per month, a laptop and a reliable internet connection, you'll be able to secure all the essentials that you need to get started. As your business grows, the expenses you need to incur might grow along with it, but the costs will never be as heavy as what you might expect from a brick and mortar establishment. Even if your business flops, you don't lose much and even better, you don't have a hefty loan to pay back regardless.

- **Product Selection** - Without having to purchase any upfront stock yourself, you're to get more room to play around in terms of product selection. Without the risk of investing in inventory that might not sell, you can dabble in a wider product selection and experiment with what your customers would like to see more of. The more customer demands you're able to cater to, the greater the opportunity to make even more profit.

- **Easily Scale Your Business** - Another perk that comes without having to invest heavily on inventory is the freedom to enjoy the more creative aspect of running a business. Those who enjoy dabbling in marketing and advertising will find this business model the perfect choice for them to actively get creative marketing and selling products that they genuinely believe in. Even better though, no matter what product you're involved in dropshipping, from something as basic as stationery supplies to heavy-duty furniture or equipment, the work that you do *remains the same*. What you're doing is acting as the middleman who transfers information back and forth between the customer and your supplier. When one supplier runs out of stock, there's always another to turn to, making this business option highly scalable.

- **The Flexibility of Working Anywhere** - Possibly one of the biggest perks with being your own boss (which you technically are if you run a dropshipping business), is the flexibility of being able to work anytime, anywhere. You could be on vacation halfway around the world and keep your business running when you've got a moment or two to spare. As we continue moving towards a more globalized world, the opportunities for you will just keep growing. You don't need to relocate to work with customers and suppliers from around the world. All you need is a good internet connection.

Dropshipping Drawbacks

Before jumping in headfirst into any kind of business, getting to know the pros and cons is the smart thing to do. Dropshipping included. It sounds easy technically, but there's more to this business model than you might initially expect. It can be quite a difficult business to maintain consistently, especially when you're starting off virtually unknown and competing with hundreds of other vendors who are doing the same thing. The day that you launch your dropshipping business you can be sure that several others are just launching their own dropshipping business too.

Drawbacks are something that no one likes to talk about, but you *need to know about it* before you get involved so you know you're walking into this venture with both eyes wide open. The last thing you want is to be taken aback by an unexpected con you didn't anticipate.

- **No High Profits with This One -** Depending on your reasons for getting into this business, the lower profit margins that come with this business model are somewhat of a problem for some entrepreneurs. If you're hoping to make millions from this business venture within the next several years, this might not be the right business model for you. You're investing less money into the business, that means you're also getting back less money than the higher-risk businesses out there. There's a lot of work that's going to be involved in keeping your business afloat and even more work and patience needed before you can turn a profit.

- **A Portion Goes to Suppliers** - For every sale that you make, a portion of your earnings is going to go towards paying your suppliers, taking your earnings down even further. After deducting the expenses needed to maintain your website, managing your orders and the effort involved in marketing and advertising your products, your profit is not something that's going to make you do cartwheels around the room in excitement. Not to mention that since profits are determined by your traffic and customer base, it might be a while before you actually *see* these profits for yourself as you work on building a steady base of clientele.

- **Tough Competition** - Competition is tough with this business model. When there's an opportunity to start a business for next to nothing, you can be sure that you're not going to be the only one who is keen to get some skin in the game. Be prepared for some tough competition, especially if your niche is one of the most popular ones. Smaller start-up businesses are sometimes forced to cut their profits by a significant amount, so they can continue offering their customers the low competitive prices that their competitors are. Bigger companies can afford to do this of course, but for smaller start-ups, cutting too much into the profit margins could mean business becomes unsustainable.

- **No Exclusivity** - With the high level of competition going around, you might not be the only vendor who's got a deal with your supplier. There's a good chance that your supplier could be working with several other vendors, selling exactly the same products you are. That's even more pressure to market your business and give your customers a reason why they should be buying from you instead.

- **Little Control** - As the middleman, you're going to have very little command over your supply-chain. You won't be able to determine the shipping times, how quickly you get to fulfill an order and even vouch for the product quality. All these aspects are out of your hands since the supplier is going to be the one who's dealing with the order fulfillment portion. If you're not someone who's comfortable relinquishing control, this might not be the ideal business option for you despite its pros.

- **Building A Brand Name Isn't Easy** - With little control over a lot of the regular management aspects that happen in business, building a brand name that's easily recognizable is not going to be easy. Even if you've sold a fantastic product to a happy customer, chances are you're not going to be remembered since it's not your logo they see being displayed on the box. Branding may not seem like a big deal until you get to a point where you want to lock in your repeat customers, which can only happen if they're loyal to your business.

- **Complications in Shipping** - Shipping on its own is not a problem. The tricky part happens when you're dealing with multiple suppliers at a time and you've got customers who are ordering items from more than just one supplier. Since the customer is ordering all the items from your shop, they would naturally expect these items to be shipped out altogether and are sometimes taken aback when being told that some items may experience delays in shipment. Some customers might be okay with it, while others are less than thrilled at this prospect. There's definitely the danger of jeopardizing your customer satisfaction levels when shipping complications come about.

- **Inventory Problems** - Delays in shipment are one

thing. What happens if your customer orders an item and then *gasp* turns out the supplier tells you it's out of stock after all. You've got to be the bearer of bad news and let the disappointed customer know that the item is not available and you'll either be left with a very disgruntled, disappointed or angry customer. Again, customer satisfaction levels could be a problem here.

- **The Cost of Your Supplier's Mistakes** - As the face of the business, the customers are going to know only you, not your supplier. Which means that any mistakes on the suppliers' end are going to end up costing you either in terms of monetary damage or damage to your reputation. Lost items, damaged products, wrong items getting shipped, delays in shipment, tracking problems, customers not getting updated about the status of their orders. All of this reflects poorly on your business and unfortunately, you're going to be the one who has to bear the cost of it all.

- **The Dangers of Fraud** - The online world is no stranger to fraud and e-commerce businesses are just as much at risk as anything else that is online. Credit card fraud, possible issues with hackers attempting to breach your security, fraudulent orders being placed by customers are just some of the many realities of running a business online that you need to contend with.

- **Underprepared for Customer Support** - Another thing that newbie entrepreneurs tend to overlook is the customer support aspect. In the excitement of wanting to scale your business, all your efforts are diverted towards trying to grow your profits and customer base. Meanwhile, the fact that more customers mean a bigger demand on providing the necessary customer support facilities gets overlooked and one of the mistakes an entrepreneur can make with any business model is to underestimate the customer support aspect.

- **When Shipping Is Too Slow** - Customers are going to become very unhappy when your products take too long to ship. No one wants to wait for an entire month or more before they finally get their hands on the item they ordered. Shipping times play a major role in a customer's decision-making process and if your competitor can offer them a much faster shipping rate, they'll instantly switch over to your competitor without so much as a second thought, even faster if that same competitor happens to offer lower shipping rates too.

The list of cons might look longer than the pros, but all things considered, dropshipping is still a good business model to consider getting your starts in, if you're well and truly prepared for what's to come. Think of it as a fantastic learning opportunity, especially when you haven't had much experience running a business of your own. You get to put your knowledge and skills to the test to see if you have what it takes to one day be an owner of an even bigger business model with greater potential. Everyone has to start somewhere, so you might as well start with something that is a relatively low risk where you don't end up losing a large chunk of your savings and getting into debt from the business loans you had to take on while you're at it.

How to Get Started with Your Dropshipping Business

The key to being successful at anything you do is to *love what you're doing.* Or at least, you should enjoy the process enough to want to wake up and do it every morning. The same principles apply when you're thinking about getting into the dropshipping business. Running this business needs to be done by going into it with the right kind of attitude and approach. If you think this is your ticket to financial freedom and making hundreds of thousands in profit, that's not the right approach. Instead, you need to approach this business by seeing it for what it is, a good side hustles with the potential to turn into something more. Not a guarantee, but a maybe.

Before you get into this business, here's what you need to give some serious thought towards:

- **No Rushing** - As excited as you may be to get your business going, jumping the gun is one of the worst things you could do. Not just with dropshipping, but any kind of business venture. That old saying *"only fools rush in"* exists for a reason, it's better to take your time and be well prepared rather than rushing the entire process because you can't wait to make something happen. Think of it this way, would you move to a new city or travel to a foreign country without at least doing some research into what you can expect? The answer is no, you wouldn't. So why would you rush this big decision to start your own business? Especially when there's money at stake. Not a lot of money, but it's still money that you worked hard for and it should be invested wisely. That's the right approach to take.

- **Saving Yourself from Overselling** - Among the many challenges an entrepreneur has to deal with, market fluctuations are one of the more unpredictable factors. Order too much and you'll run into the risk of being overstocked, order too little and you will equally put yourself at risk of being under stocked. This is where dropshipping comes in handy, to mitigate that risk by letting the supplier hold onto the entire inventory while you only pay them per order. This approach is particularly useful when it comes to seasonal products, where demand only spikes maybe once or twice a year and nothing more. In this way, dropshipping is safeguarding you from the uncertainties of the retail space and saving you a lot of money in the process.

- **Don't Forget About Your Research** - Market research is crucial to the success of any business, even a considerably small scale business like dropshipping. In fact, dropshipping could be *used as market research itself*. Let's assume that you had a much bigger, long-term goal of running your own business that you could one day turn into a household name. Maybe even a business empire. You've got the skills, knowledge and the resources to do it, but you're still not sure if it's a good idea to stock up on inventory where there's still a 50/50 chance it may not get sold, despite the research you've done. In this case, dropshipping can be used as a means to an end, a tool which can be used to help mitigate the risks involved. Test the waters and see if there is demand for the product that you intend to sell and use dropshipping as a way to do it. There's a lot of benefits going with this approach, one of them being that you don't risk a lot of your own money doing actual market research via dropshipping and the other being that you'll get a much better gauge about what the market demand is really like instead of just making educated guesses and predictions based on the research and the numbers you've gathered. You'll be able to text just how quickly stock moves in a month, how frequently customers are making repeat purchases, how much they're willing to pay for an item, how much you could price your item at and still make a sale and you'll find out if it is viable to invest in the products that you want after all.

That is just one small part of the preparation process that gets you ready to take on the dropshipping retail space. There are several other areas you need to look into before you can even launch your business and be ready to take on customers' orders as soon as they come in. Before you get started, here's what else you need to look into to make sure all your bases are covered:

- Do your own due diligence and research, research, research. Do a deep dive into what type of products would be the best fit for the kind of business, target market, strategy and long-term business goals that you have in mind.

- Do even more research into your customer demographics.

Learn everything you need to know about them: from what kind of products they search for online to how much time they spend online browsing through retail sites to find what they're looking for.

- Do research into who your competitors are. What are they doing to win customers? What type of products are they selling and how are they doing it better than you are? How much are they pricing their products for? Do they offer free shipping options? What are their customer reviews like? Do so much research, until you know them like the back of your hand.

- Keep searching until you find the perfect supplier. The one who is the best fit for your business and has all the criteria that you're looking for. Don't stop until you've found the one and avoid settling for a supplier that you're less than happy working with because you're eager to get your business going.

- Figure out your marketing strategy and how you intend to promote these products. To drive sales and traffic to your platform, you need to put yourself out there and ensure that the most important customers are sitting up and taking notice. What details are you going to include in your product description and why should your customers buy from you instead of your competitors? Are your reasons compelling enough to stand out?

What's My Product?

Moving onto the next area that you should be looking into before launching your dropshipping business. The products that you intend to sell. There are definitely going to be some dropshippers who start off not quite knowing what they should sell. They just want to start some kind of business of their own to learn the ropes and that's perfectly okay. You might find an idea or inspiration for what products you should be specializing in down the road. If you have no clue what kind of products you should be selling as a start, choose to start with something simple that can be sold easily. Novelty, cute, artistic t-shirts for example, or shopper bags that support a charity or a cause. Coffee mugs with amusing, somewhat funny descriptions written on them, or even some motivational merchandise with words of wisdom to inspire others. Inexpensive jewelry could be a good option, although that is mostly catered towards the female customer base. The idea is to focus on selling items that are inexpensive, but attractive enough to garner a sale as something to start with. You can always expand or change your products later on once you've gained more experience.

What's My Niche?

After you've been doing this for a while and you think you've got a pretty good idea about how dropshipping works so far, consider looking into finding your niche instead. Having a store that specializes in a specific niche type of product is going to make it easier for your customers to associate with you. When you need sports clothing and equipment, for example, you automatically think Adidas or Nike and you know just where to go to get those items. You wouldn't go searching for those products in a store that is selling all sorts of miscellaneous general items together with sports clothing because you're unlikely to find what you're looking for. As a customer yourself, if you would rather buy the items you need at a store you know can be trusted to provide quality products, you can be sure that many of your customers will be thinking along the same lines.

Choosing to narrow down your focus may seem like a counterproductive idea since you want to aim to make as much profit as possible, but if you put the effort into being the best in your niche, you'll quickly start to gain traction among customers as they become familiar with your store. You want your customers to associate your store with being the go-to place for the specific items that they need, just like Nike and Adidas have done. Having customer loyalty and repeat purchases could give your dropshipping business the needed profit boost.

Here are some of the advantages to consider which might convince you why having a niche product base could be a good idea after all:

- You give yourself a competitive advantage against big giants like eBay and Amazon, who often lack the necessary customer friendly approach because they have so much going on. You, as the not-so-giant store, can use that to your advantage, adding the missing human touch element to your business, which can go a long way in making you memorable in the eyes of your customer.

- Knowing who your audience demographic is, it's much easier when you have less to focus on. When you're able to focus on your customers, crafting the right kind of advertising material that gets noticed is easier to do. It's like having a conversation. When you know who exactly it is that you're talking to, you know just what you need to say to sway them over to your side.

- Another advantage of knowing your audience is the ability to design better-focused marketing plans. If you've got big ideas about how to scale your business, having a specific niche to focus on makes the steps that you need to take to achieve those goals much clearer.

- Not to mention that SEO is now easier to handle too when you know what keywords should be used to reach out to the group of customers you're zoning in on. Getting noticed online has a lot to do with SEO and utilizing the right keywords in your descriptions or hashtags. All the content in your store and marketing material needs to be SEO-friendly, a task which is almost impossible to achieve in a store which sells a general mishmash of products because you're not having anything specific to focus on. A niche, on the other hand, will conveniently let you drop just the right keywords needed to boost your page to the very top of Google's results page, just what you need to get right in front of your online customers.

What Products Should I NOT Sell?

Some products are not the right fit for the dropshipping world. The complications involved with the shipping and the customs regulations you might have to deal with will seriously impact whether a certain product is worth all the time and energy you're investing in it. Dropshipping products is easy since the supplier handles the hard part for you, but dropshipping the wrong type of products could land you in more trouble than the products are worth.

Some examples of products that are not such a good idea for the dropshipping business include products which:

- **Are Too Heavy** - The heavier the item, the more expensive it is to ship, which then makes the delivery a lot more difficult to manage and not to mention expensive. Customers are not going to be very happy either, about having to deal with high shipping fees, even though they know that they need your items.

- **Are Fragile** - The risk of the products getting broken en route to the customer is too high and not worth it, considering that profit margins are already low as it is with dropshipping.

- **Deal with Copyright Issues** - It's too much of a legal mess to deal with products that might have copyright issues or infringement. Knock-off items may seem like no big deal, but they can pose a whole host of legal problems that you simply don't want to get involved in. Not to mention the damage that it could do to your business's reputation whenever there's a legal problem that the customers get wind of.

- **Are Too Technical** - It's never a good idea to buy any kind of gadgets or technical products online. These items usually don't come cheap and you want to test them out, preferably in store, before you spend that kind of money taking them home. Buying online eliminates the possibility of being able to determine that you're getting the best gadget in the store since you have no control over what's going to arrive at your customer's doorstep. They are not going to be very happy receiving faulty or broken products and even products that fail to live up to its promise on your website. There are too many risks involved with dropshipping these types of items and it's best to stay away from them altogether.

What's My Payment Gateway?

Customers these days want options. They don't want just one choice of payment method available, they want to know they have a choice to go with the payment option they prefer. Some customers may not want to pay with credit cards, while others prefer to pay with credit cards as their first choice. Other customers might like the idea of using PayPal instead of their debit cards. Customers prefer to go with the option they believe they can trust the most and it is up to you to provide them with these options on your website.

Setting up payment gateways which are secure and stable enough is a crucial aspect that you need to look into. Important factors that need to be considered with this one include:

- Ensure that your payment gateways are going to be accepting all major forms of credit and debit card options, including Visa and MasterCard and American Express. Don't forget about the PayPal options too.

- Checking if your payment gateway is going to be accessible in your country and other international countries where your customers may be residing.

- Is your choice of payment gateway going to offer international currency support? Because if it doesn't, it needs to, your customers are not going to be based in one location alone.

- Making comparisons with the transaction fees involved. Avoid being tempted to go for what's the lowest cost and instead choose to go for something that is secure.

Am I Trustworthy?

Reputation is everything in business and your customers are going to feel a lot better about buying from you if they know that they can trust you. Understandably, trust can be a difficult thing to come by when your customers have never met you in person, but there is something that enhances the trust your customer feels when they peruse your store. The feedback and customer reviews left by others who have made purchases from you in the past.

Based on research which was conducted in 2015, turns out that 70% of consumers are more than likely to search online for product reviews before they make a purchase. If the reviews on your site are favorable, you increase your chances of drawing in new customers who have convinced by the praises left behind by customers in the past. It is important that you do what you can to enhance your online reputation too. When a customer leaves a comment, return the favor by thanking them for taking the time to do so and that you hope they're happy with their purchase. If a customer leaves a negative review, do everything that you can to address the problem and make sure it has been sorted. Never leave a negative review unattended or ignored, make it a point to respond to every comment, both good and bad. That's how you retain good customer service.

Chapter 3: The First Few Steps

Dropshipping commands more than 30% of today's e-commerce industry. It's fantastic as a low-risk business, but it can be tough to achieve significant success due to the low-profit margins you're working with. Competition is tough and you have to really narrow down your focus, both in terms of which niche markets you intend to target and the type of platform you want to use to run your business, to see significant results.

Dropshipping Platforms

As the industry continues to grow and expand, so too do the opportunities and options that you have to work with. The beauty of the digital age is that you're spoilt for choice and you'll never be restricted to only one method or approach to doing something, including running an online business. Every successful business that you see today was built on a firm foundation that encompassed several factors which eventually contributed to the success of the business. For dropshipping, that foundation building begins with choosing the right dropshipping platform to work with that is going to help you realize all the goals you set out to achieve when you decided to get started.

The first few steps before you begin your business include three major phases:

- Step #1 - Deciding on your dropshipping platform
- Step #2 - Selecting your niche
- Step #3 - Finding the right suppliers for your business

Once you're ready to get going, there are several well-established dropshipping platforms that you could look into:

Amazon FBA

Fulfilled by Amazon (FBA) is the perfect choice for the savvy and ambitious entrepreneur who has their sights fixed on catering to a much larger target customer base. If this is part of your dropshipping business goals, then you're going to find this platform the perfect fit. The business scalability options that come with Amazon FBA are impressive and it goes without saying that the platform's reputation precedes it. Customers trust the products that they're getting from Amazon and that trust leads to them making purchases through Amazon FBA rather than taking a risk with an unknown vendor.

Amazon FBA offers vendors with more capital to spend the option of stocking inventory in their warehouses, which means the platform keeps your items for you until such time when an order is made. They will then proceed to ship the item out to the customers on your behalf. What's unique about using Amazon FBA as your dropshipping platform is that your items will be eligible for the shipping promotions, like Amazon Prime and its Free Super Saver Shipping options, which entice customers even more. They can rarely resist the option of free shipping.

Amazon has been around for a long time and it has already established a reputation for itself as being among the top online retail platforms for trusted, quality products. Choosing to list your items on this platform means you're benefiting from Amazon's existing pool of customers, some of whom are repeat customers, thereby increasing your chances of making a sale. Another advantage with Amazon FBA is the replacement and returns policy that the platform has already set in place, further cementing the fact that they take their commitment to providing great service very seriously. This is a significant advantage if you hope to retain and even build customer loyalty down the road because customers want to know that you take their concerns into consideration and listen to them.

With the trust factor in play, you'll have the advantage of being able to see your products on Amazon for a slightly higher profit margin compared to if you were to do it on your own. Customers are more comfortable paying the asking price when they know they're dealing with a company or a business that they can trust, something they may not be as willing to do on less established websites in case they get cheated or scammed out of their money.

Since Amazon is going to take care of the inventory and the shipping process for you, that leaves you with more time on your hands to think about managing all the other aspects of your business and focus on your customer service efforts.

Yahoo Store

It may not be as big a name like Amazon, but Yahoo reputation is strong enough to serve its purpose. At least when you mention Yahoo, most customers are familiar with the name and associate it as a reputable brand, much like they do with Amazon. Yahoo Store works the same way as most other dropshipping platforms, where you as the vendor would need to create an account before you can start adding products to your store. One advantage with this platform is that it integrates several shipping options and accepts most payment types.

Unlike Amazon FBA though, Yahoo Store's inventory management is a little tricky until you've learned to get the hang of it. It is worth considering this platform if what you're looking for is the peace of mind knowing that your business is secure and that if you need help, you would simply need to pick up the phone or shoot them a quick email any time of day.

Shopify

Next to Amazon, Shopify is probably the next best platform when it comes to dropshipping based on popularity. With over 500,000+ active stores on Shopify and counting, this is one platform to consider after Amazon FBA. Shopify was acquired by Oberlo back in 2016 and since then, Oberlo has made it much easier to fulfill orders via this platform with its plugin tool that makes the process a lot simpler.

Shopify's popularity is thanks to largely to its extremely user-friendly features, especially for vendors who are starting their own dropshipping websites for the very first time. Sign up, log in and follow all the step-by-step instructions and you're good to go. One fantastic benefit that Shopify offers its users is the 24-hour customer support that is easily contactable through email, phone or even virtual chat, depending on what your preference is. The platform also provides a forum for users to easily find the help topics that they're looking for and where other users can get together to exchange and share information, help other users navigate the platform and even divulge insightful tips to help make the platform's experience much better.

Shopify's features are great, but they do come at a cost which starts anywhere from $29 dollars, with the most expensive option being $299. New vendors are encouraged to go for the basic, more affordable option to start with until your business has gained some traction, and then you can look into upgrading your services as needed. Shopify also provides a more premium service known as Advanced Shopify, which is home to many of the current top performing stores. Once your business has picked up and developed a strong enough reputation, you could consider upgrading to Shopify's premium service if it suits your current business needs.

Oberlo

After acquiring Shopify, Oberlo quickly made a name for itself as one of the world's leaders in online retail and marketplace. Oberlo helps vendors connect with their suppliers, the ones who are in charge of shipping the products out to the customer.

The only drawback with Oberlo is that it only works on Shopify's platform. This platform also has the option of a free account, but the downside with that is you'll only be limited to 500 items for sale on your platform and only 50 orders a month. The limitation is, of course, going to affect how much profit you'll be making in a month, but you do have a choice to upgrade to the paid option, which starts from $29.90 a month and upwards, depending on what package you take.

WooCommerce

Aside from Shopify, you'll come across WooCommerce as another widely used e-commerce regular for dropshipping purposes. WooCommerce is used worldwide and a major contributing factor to its popularity is the fact that the platform is not only easy to use but is free too. To set up and account and start selling with WooCommerce, you'll need to install and go. Running on WordPress, users of WooCommerce will have the advantage of getting access to multiple add-ons for free.

BigCommerce

Another contender in the dropshipping is BigCommerce, a hosted platform that currently hosts roughly 50,000 small business websites and counting and more than 2,000 enterprise companies. It's simple user interface and ease of use is a big reason why the platform has quickly managed to cement a name for itself and compared to a lot of the other established platforms, BigCommerce is easily the more affordable option when it doesn't charge its users a fee for transactions.

Another perk with using BigCommerce is the unlimited discounts that the platform offers its staff. You're also able to get almost the same type of customer service and support that you would with platforms like Shopify. BigCommerce is growing in popularity and with many big-name companies like Toyota, Skull Candy, Camelbak and more already calling the platform home, a starting price of $29 is not a bad price to pay for a platform with promise and potential.

Magento

Magento is a powerful e-commerce site for the more advanced, tech-savvy dropshippers since is complex interface might not be something beginners are keen on if they're looking for something that is easy to use and doesn't involve too much hassle. To successfully use this platform, you're going to need at least some basic knowledge of computer programming or you might find it a struggle. Most of the dropshippers you're going to find here are either those who are already well-versed in the platform's store development, or they have the budget needed to hire a program developer on their team who specifically handles that aspect of the business.

Given its more advanced features, starting a dropshipping business on this site might require that you handle some troubleshooting issues when it comes to updating the platform or trying to resolve any errors. This is not the platform for you if you're a beginner, or have little to no knowledge about software and programming.

Despite being challenging to use though, Magento has still acquired quite a crowd on its platform and has a dedicated team of developers and software designers who are on hand to help newbies to space. They are even YouTube channels available, along with forums and blogs where users can seek help should they run into any problems with the platform.

Magento is a free platform and if you've got a little help on your side, you'll be able to launch your dropshipping store quickly and start making sales.

OpenCart

Another e-commerce platform that comes for free is OpenCart, but unlike Magento, this one is easy enough to set up without requiring any overly complex tech knowledge. The platform is free, but you will have to pay for hosting it, which is still inexpensive. Designed for e-commerce use, OpenCart offers users all the necessary dropshipping essentials like having a dashboard, analytics and even order volume data with the added benefit of being easy to use.

Getting onto this platform is free and users have the option of choosing from any of its multiple paid or free themes and plugins for their dropshipping use. Once you've got an account on the platform, you'll be able to access their forums and email them for support if you're facing any difficulties trying to set up your store.

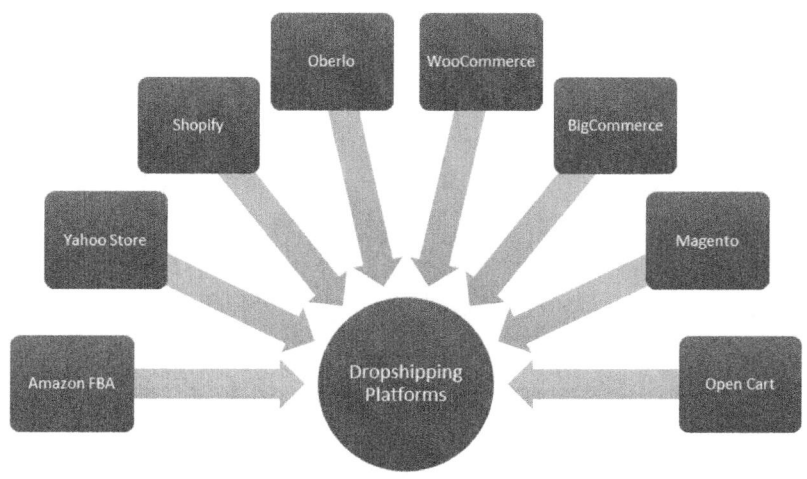

Popular Dropshipping Platforms

Picture 3

Other Dropshipping Related Sites That Prove Useful

Aside from these big-name platforms, here are some other dropshipping websites and directories that you might find useful for your business:

- **AliExpress** - A name that many are familiar with, AliExpress is both a dropshipping and wholesale platform that connects suppliers and products to the dropshipping who is searching for what they have to offer. The platform already boasts an impressive range of more than a million products, coming from suppliers in over 40 different niche categories and counting. AliExpress is slowly becoming a household name and the go-to place for affordable products with a wide range to choose from.

- **SaleHoo** - Another platform which helps to connect the dropshippers to the right suppliers is SaleHoo. Connecting suppliers that service niches in the United States, Australia and the United Kingdom, SaleHoo is going to be one of the most powerful research tools that are going to save you countless hours in time-consuming research. At a cost of $67 annually, the price tag seems a little steep, but at least you'll know that if you don't like what you paid for, you can cash in on their 60-day promise of giving you your money back.

- **Worldwide Brands** - If you're looking for a comprehensive directory where all the bulk distributors and the dropshippers come together in one easy, convenient location, look no further than Worldwide Brands. The site continuously updates the listings on their page, so there's always going to be new suppliers or new niches to discover. In case you're worried about the reliability aspect of it, Worldwide Brands does its part to ensure the sites listed are reliable.

- **Wholesale 2B** - With the lowest prices guaranteed from dropshippers and over a million products to choose from, dropshipping has never been easier than with Wholesale 2B. Vendors come here to pick their products to be sold on Amazon, BigCommerce, Shopify and eBay, so you can rest assured that you're not getting any dodgy products that will end up wasting your money.

- **National Dropshippers** - The website sells an impressive variety of products which range from barbeque grills to something as small as umbrellas. With more than 250,000 products for sale, National Dropshippers offers its users a $19.99 monthly service cost, while dropshipping costs are $2.49 for every order.

Dropshipping Websites for Sale

Not every entrepreneur is keen on starting something directly from scratch, even a dropshipping business. Understandable, given that starting businesses - any kind of business for that matter - from the ground up is no easy task, even if it is a considerably simple business model like dropshipping. All businesses are hard work and if starting a dropshipping business from scratch sounds too stressful, why not consider buying an existing business and taking over the reins from there?

Sounds like something you're more comfortable with? Well, then you'll be pleased to know that there are several websites you could scour to search for an existing business to buy. Some of these platforms include:

- **Flippa** is where you can find just about any kind of online business, from general e-commerce stores to dropshipping websites. Any business that the internet can think of, you'll be likely to find here on Flippa. Since its inception in 2009, the platform has experienced favorable success, establishing a credible name for itself within the industry. A quick search online will reveal the positive feedback that Flippa has received from those who have used this service. Before the popular Facebook platform that we know today existed, founder Mark Zuckerberg was running "Facemash", which was also sold on Flippa.

- **Exchange Market Place,** which is a well-established dropshipping marketplace online and has seen many dropshipping businesses being bought and sold since it first began.

- **E-commerce Pro** lets you purchase a dropshipping website which has already been built. As soon as you've made that final purchase, you'll be ready to start running your platform almost immediately, bypassing all the hassle that you need to go through in the early stages with market research, finding a niche category, searching for suppliers and more because everything is already taken care of by Ecommerce Pro.

- **Drop Ship for Sale** lets you buy a dropshipping website and then run it the same way that you would with an online store. The site makes it easy for you to select the dropshipping websites that you want based on niche categories and within less than 24-hours of finding something that you like, you could be up and running with your very own business underway.

- **WooDropship** is another popular site to search for your next business venture, but this one works a little differently from the other sites selling existing dropshipping businesses. With WooDropship, what you're getting is a service that helps you *build* your online website. Give them all the necessary details regarding your business, including what your niche is and your preferred method of payment and they'll take it from there. Within the next 48-hours, your website is ready to launch and once your website has been built, it belongs entirely to you.

How to Find the Best Niches

After you've decided on the dropshipping platform that's going to be the best fit for you and your business, it's time to move onto Step #2 of the foundation building process. Finding your niche. Your niche here is going to be the group of customers that you intend to target. Who do you intend to sell your products to and why do they need them? How will you reach these customers and is there enough of a demand to sustain your business? If you've got a specific product or two that you're passionate about selling, how do you combine that passion to meet the needs of the niche market you plan to target? Is this a strong enough niche to help you make some money?

They key to success with finding your niche is to choose the niche that you have a genuine interest in *while simultaneously* being a niche that is profitable and in demand too. Working on that middle ground, combining the best of both worlds is the key to keeping your business sustainable. Do your research into which products are in demand the most, based on popularity and out of these products which ones are the most profitable. From there, you can then focus your efforts into choosing the products that interest you the most.

Another way to find a niche is to do some research based on keywords. Make a list of the keywords which are going to be relevant to your product and once you're done, type these keywords into Google's Keyword Planner for a clearer picture about the kind of search volume these keywords are getting. For example, if you wanted to sell pet supplies on your website, some of the relevant keywords on your list would be "dog food", "dog kibbles" "cat food", "harness", "collar", or "pet shampoo". However, you may find upon checking with Google's Keyword Planner though, that "dog food" might be getting more searches than "dog kibbles" do. This way, you'll be able to prioritize which keywords should take precedence in your product description and work from there.

With making the final decision about what your niche should be, there are several considerations you want to keep in mind to help you with the selection process:

- **It's Not a Rushed Process** - You cannot rush into selecting the perfect niche any more than you can rush starting your own business. The right niche is going to be the one that either makes or breaks your business, so take as much time as you need to be sure that you're making the right choice.

- **Observing the Competition** - Who are your primary competitors for the niche that you're about to choose and are they doing well? If your niche has far too many competitors already, it might be best to think about choosing another niche to go with just to be on the safe side. You don't want to put your business at risk of being drowned out or overshadowed, which will happen since you're the newcomer and they've been around for a while. If your competitors are already well-established, built a credible reputation for themselves and have a loyal following of customers, it might be tough to break into that circle and gain traction.

- **Profit Per Sale** - A passion for entrepreneurship may be one thing, but let's face it, money is one of the major reasons many people get into business in the first place. For the opportunity to make money and how much profit you will be able to make with every sale needs to be a factor for consideration when you're selecting your niche. Choosing a niche with a higher purchase price gives you your best chance at making a nice profit margin that could range anywhere from 15% to 20%, depending on the product you're selling. Another option to boost your profit margins is to consider a more diverse inventory selection, while still making sure that you're sticking to the relevant niche that you've selected.

- **Thinking About Future Trends** - Now that you've found something that seems to tick all the right boxes, here's another question you need to consider. Will this product continue to be in demand moving forward? What are the predictions for the future demand trend with what you're about to sell? Conducting a quick search on Google Trends will provide some insightful information into this area, particularly in regards to how popular your keywords are likely to remain over a certain period.

- **Think About Seasonality** - Something that often gets overlooked when selecting a niche is whether the product you intend to sell is seasonal or not. Is this something that is going to be needed by your customers throughout the year? Or only maybe one or twice throughout the year? If it is seasonal, how much profit are you likely to make during peak demand periods and is it enough to offset the rest of the year when sales might be lower?

- **Think About Repeat Purchases** - Another aspect that gets overlooked is whether your customers are likely to make repeat purchases with the products that you intend to sell. Selling items which are consumable or perishable for example will give you greater potential for consistent profits if your customers have to repeatedly buy them when they run out of stock.

Here's what a good niche and a bad niche would look like:

- **Good Niche:**
    - Products with a lot of options
    - Products with variation
    - Products that customers need to make repeat purchases of
    - Products which are customizable
    - Products which are unique enough that customers don't mind waiting for (like furniture)

- **Bad Niche:**
    - Products which are personalized too much

(bedding or clothing)
- Products with expiration dates (seasonal products)
- Products that have a strong emotional attachment to them
- Products which can cause technical or customer service problems (electronics)

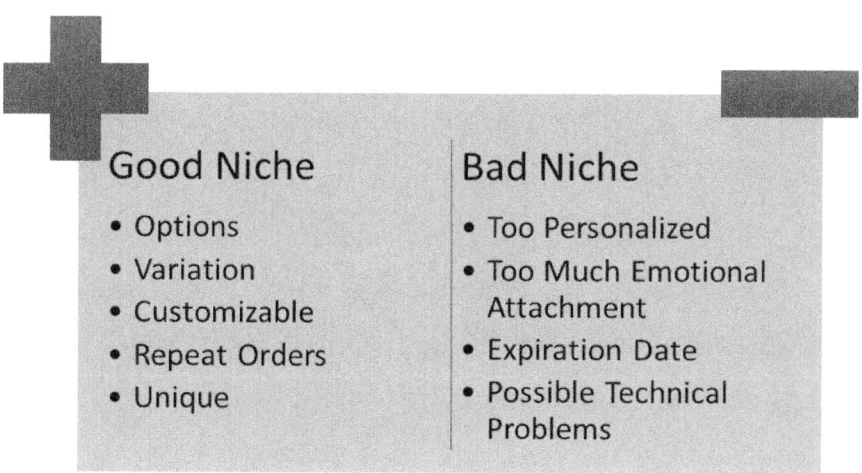

Good Niche Products vs. Bad Niche Products

Picture 4

How to Find Your Suppliers

Now for Step #3 of the foundation building process. Finding the right suppliers to work with. It is very crucial that you get this step absolutely right because getting stuck with unprofessional suppliers can be nothing short of disastrous for your business. Choose the wrong suppliers and your business is going to fail even before it has had a chance to succeed. Sounds like there's a lot of pressure involved in this step, but it cannot be emphasized enough just how important it is that you build a great working relationship with suppliers whom you can trust.

When searching for the right suppliers for your business, there are several factors that need to be considered in this phase:

- Finding your suppliers might be a bit of a challenge. In general, suppliers don't usually go around marketing themselves to dropshipping vendors, so it is up to you to go searching for them. Since they don't market themselves much, this might take a while to do.

- Be prepared for most (if not all) of your suppliers to be based in Asia. Most products are made in Asia, so it would make sense that many of the suppliers would be based in this region too. Although they conduct business internationally, the language barrier would still be a bit of a problem that you *might* need to prepare for.

- You're going to have to be prepared to do more research yet again with sourcing your suppliers, especially if you intend to work with overseas suppliers. You're going to have to do some thorough digging into what sort of material is used to make your products, how quickly they're able to deliver as well as what their return policies are, just to name a few.

- It's best if you could contact these suppliers directly since you need to develop a genuine working relationship with them. Even better if you could meet them in person, although this may not be entirely possible if you're working with an overseas supplier. Making direct contact is the quickest way to get all your questions answered before you decide if this is the supplier that you want to commit to. A professional supplier should be more than happy to accommodate your requests and answer any questions you may have.

- If your supplier is willing, it would be great if they could provide you with the contact details of some of their past or current customers. You could reach out to them and see what their experience has been like working with this supplier and if they would go on to recommend the services of the supplier to others.

- Reach out to a few of the different suppliers you've narrowed down on your list and see if they would be willing to send you samples of the products that you intend to sell. It's best to get a sample before you begin selling so you can be confident about the quality of the product that you're selling. You'll also be able to see for yourself just how quickly their shipping process takes, the sort of packaging that they use and what their customer service is like. This is the best way to get a first-hand view of what your customer is going to be experiencing. If you're not happy with it, they won't be happy with it either.

- Order some product samples from your competitors too and compare the quality of their items against the sample items that you received from your supplier. Is it comparable? Or is the quality of your competitors' products better? What about the shipping times and the delivery fee incurred? If your competitors' products are better, you might consider reaching out to their supplier and see if they would be willing to work with you too. Ordering samples from several of your competitors is a way of doing market research so you can determine for yourself which aspects of your business may need improving on. Never skimp on the quality that you provide to your customers. If they don't like what you're selling and it's not at least comparable or better than your competitors, they're not going to come back to your store again.

- The benefit of using a domestic supplier to fulfill your orders is the possibility of quicker delivery times since there is a much shorter supply chain to contend with. Choosing to work with a domestic supplier also gives you a greater chance of being able to conduct quality inspections, since you'll most likely be able to meet with them directly and see the products for yourself. Shipping rates also tend to be cheaper without having to deal with customs or import tariffs.

Dropshipping Suppliers to Stay Away From

Suppliers are the backbone of every single dropshipping business that is currently running online today. Without the suppliers, you would have no business because there would be nothing to sell. Finding the right supplier can be hard since you won't know exactly if they are going to live up to everything that they've promised until you've been working with them for a while.

However, there are certain red flag signs that warn you a supplier should be avoided and it's not just based on bad reviews and poor quality products alone. The indicators of a supplier that is going to be bad for your business include:

- If the supplier is charging a higher than average pre-order fees. It is normal for fees to either increase slightly if the order is complex, or decrease if you're ordering in bulk, but when the fees are higher than what they should be, that's a supplier you want to stay away from.

- If they insist on being paid a monthly fee, or even an ongoing fee, just to do business with them.

- If the supplier is unprofessional right from the start and has poor communication skills. If they take far too long to respond to your emails or phone calls, that's never a good sign.

- If the supplier is not willing to charge a minimum order fee to be able to fulfill the orders as soon as they come in. For example, if the supplier you're working with has a minimum order of 50 units, you'll pay for the 50 units upfront but the supplier will fulfill the orders immediately when they come in from your store. Suppliers who are not willing to do this are better suited for wholesale dropshipping.

Chapter 4: Get Clicking and Start Building

Deciding on your platform, niche and sourcing your suppliers was the first part of setting up your dropshipping venture. The next part is going to focus on building a reliable, professional looking website that will start driving business in and get your products moving.

You may not have a physical shop and you may not hold any of the actual stock, but you still need a website to run your business and this is why.

Is A Dropshipping Website Necessary?

Yes, it is. Despite the small profit margins, there is still potential in this business model, but you need a good website to achieve this. Since neither you nor your supplier is going to have any direct contact with the customer and vice versa, your website is going to be the only link that will bridge the gap between you and the customer.

In fact, having a website is going to boost your credibility not just among your customers, but among the suppliers too.

Suppliers want to work with someone who means business and even better if they already have an existing website that they're keen to launch. When a supplier sees your website, it's easier to convince them that you mean business and that you're serious about developing a business partnership with them to move their products. It's like going for a job interview and your website is your resume. Go in with a blank resume and you're not going to be as convincing. If the supplier was your employer, they'd be wondering why they should consider working with you when there are other vendors out there, some who are already more established even with an existing customer base. You need to have something to show and that something is your website.

Your competitors are going to have websites and if you don't, that puts you at a significant disadvantage. Your customers will be expecting a website if you run a business, especially when it's done online where you need to look convincing and legitimate to avoid being thought of as a scam.

A website gives your business the credibility it needs to survive in the online space and if you're running an online business, you need a place to showcase all your products for sale. Customers want shipping to be made as easy, straightforward and as convenient as possible. They don't want to go to multiple locations to find what they need. They want a one-stop shop that is going to service all their requirements from start to finish. You need a website to be able to do all of that so yes, it is safe to say that dropshipping is a necessary component for your business. Your niche customers need to know where and how to find you and they can't do that online without a proper website.

There are benefits that come with having your very own website for the dropshipping business you intend to run too. First thing, having a website that is completely your own gives you the freedom and the luxury of being able to have full creative control over what content goes onto your website. You're essentially your own boss and your website can contain anything that you want it to. You have the freedom to list as many products as you like and you can list *any* product that you like. Everything is entirely up to you.

Having a professional looking site is among the many contributing factors that will ultimately lead to a sale. Thinking like a customer, wouldn't you prefer to buy from a website that looks legitimate? Utilizing the available themes and plugins that come with certain platforms, there's a lot that you can do to spruce up your site and it costs very little to do so compared to having a physical business where you would need to spend money on renovations and maintenance. The cost of running a website is next to nothing if you think about it, which is why dropshipping is one of *the most* affordable business models you will find.

Creating a Website for Your Online Business

If you're not particularly tech-savvy, the idea of setting up your own website might be causing you to panic a little right now. Where would you even begin and how are you going to set up something that looks as good as your competitors when you have no idea where to begin. Don't worry; it's not going to be as tough as it sounds. A lot of newcomers to the online business world tend to worry about the setting up a website portion of the process, so you're not alone in this. Contrary to what you might think, you don't need a lot of tech-related or programming experience to be able to set up something impressive, all you need is a good step-by-step guide to lead you through the process.

Website development has gone through a lot of change over the past few years to accommodate the boom of online retail which has grown at an exponential rate over the years, making it easier than ever for just about anyone to build a website. With a good guide and a little patience, you'll be able to set something up before you know it and here's where you begin:

- **Step 1: Choosing A Platform -** Some website building platforms and companies are offering services which provide you with the templates that you need to start designing your own website from scratch. They have simplified the process even more by providing specific instructions every step of the way, guiding you easy to follow instructions throughout the template. All you need to do is fill in the blank spaces with the relevant information. Some companies even offer to do it all for you if needed, for a fee of course. Among the popular platforms of choice, today include WordPress, Shopify, WooCommerce, Wix, BigCommerce, Weebly, Magento, SquareSpace, Volusion and more, each platform coming in at various pricing models and each with their strengths and benefits of their own, depending on the features that you're after.

- **Step 2: Domain Names** - A domain name is a name that is going to appear after "www." on your website. Your domain name should ideally be something simple, short, easy to remember and easy to spell. It also needs to be relevant to the business that you're doing so your customers can make the connection between the domain name and your business. Creating confusion among customers is never a good thing, you'll put your business at risk of losing them if they're put off by how complicated or messy your set-up seems to be. With customers, it's always best to keep it as simple and easy as possible. Domain names are generally affordable, so it should be factored into the cost of setting up your business right from the start.

- **Step 3: Hosting Your Website -** Hosting means your website is live and online on the world-wide-web. You're basically letting the whole world know that your business exists and it's right here for them to discover on the internet. Depending on who your host provider is, there's going to be a fee incurred but again, it's pretty inexpensive all things considered. Most hosting platforms require an annual fee for their services and some of the more popular hosting platforms include the likes of GoDaddy and BlueHost. When choosing your host provider, you always want to go for servers which have fantastic customer reviews from its existing pool of customers. You'll also want to choose a host that comes with fast servers.

- **Step 4: Building It -** The building part is going to depend on which platform you decide to go with. Choosing Shopify, for example, means that you'll need to sign up for an account and then choosing from one of their pricing plans. Shopify's team will then work on building your online store for you, but you'll be able to customize it according to what you want. Other platforms like WooCommerce for example, require WordPress installation first before the WooCommerce plugin can be used. Other platforms like Weebly, Wix, BigCommerce and Magento however, only provide you with a template layout on their site for you to edit and customize as you see fit. Customize your store according to theme, content and logo placement, structure, number of pages, how many categories there will be plugins, widgets and more.

- **Step 5: Installing WordPress and WooCommerce** - The installation process should take no more than 5-minutes to get done, depending on how fast your internet speed is. Once that's done, create your account so you're now the administrator and you can start managing your dropshipping website. After that's completed, the next step is to install your WooCommerce plugin and your WooCommerce store to begin setting up the rest of your website functions, including payments, cart, product pages, currency, checkout and more.

- **Step 6: Picking Your Theme** - Time to pick a theme that is going to entice your customers and draw them to your store. The theme that you choose will determine how your website is going to look overall, so pick a good one.

- **Step 7: Time to Fill It Up** - Time to fill your website up with beautiful images and detailed descriptions of the products you intend to sell. Since you're not going to have any physical stock of the product, you'll have to ask the supplier to provide you with the best images that they have of the products you plan to sell.

7 Steps to Building Your Dropshipping Website

Picture 5

Why Choose BlueHost?

This reputable company has been in business for a while now and based on their customer reviews, they've been doing extremely well. Since it first began, BlueHost has today grown to host more than 2 million websites and counting and over 850,000 blogs and this is on a global scale. For those who choose the WooCommerce or WordPress platform options, BlueHost has even made it easier to seamlessly integrate the installation process with a few simple clicks.

The platform's uptime rate is guaranteed at 99.9%, so you'll be able to operate with peace of mind knowing that your dropshipping site isn't going to be slowing down anytime soon.

Other than the amount of time and stress you're going to save, thanks to how easy it is to use its services, other reasons why you should consider BlueHost as your host of choice includes:

- It's a company that is well established.
- Excellent 24/7 customer service support.
- It offers free domain names.
- WordPress recommends BlueHost officially and it comes pre-installed on WordPress already.
- The company offers SSL certificates for free.

Best of all, if you're not satisfied with the services you've experienced so far, BlueHost offers a 30-day guarantee or your money back.

How Do I Know If My Dropshipping Website Is Any Good?

Creating anything great is going to take time, including your website. Take your time with this, because you want to end up with a site that looks so appealing even you would want to shop on it. There are several factors that contribute towards making a dropshipping website what it is and for yours to stand out and make an impression on your online audience; your website needs to contain the following elements:

- **Have A Title -** Each product listed on your site must have a title. It is important that the right keywords are used in your title so search engines like Google, Yahoo and Bing can easily detect them based on their algorithm and your website turns up on their search results page. This is how customers get to know about you.

- **Have A Description -** The more details and information you include about your product, the more convinced your customers will be as to why they should purchase your products. Again, remember to include as many keywords and phrases as possible so the search engines don't miss it.

- **Label Your Bestsellers -** Making your best-selling products easily accessible to your customers lets them know which products they should be keeping their eyes on too. When new customers see how popular a product is, they'll be convinced that this product must be worth the purchase and they'll be more likely to buy it too.

- **Include Reviews by Customers -** Lend credibility to your products and services by making honest customer reviews transparent and out there for other new customers to see.

A Good Dropshipping Website
Picture 6

How to Scale Your Business

Any entrepreneur who starts off has dreams of scaling their business to greater heights one day. To fulfill that dream of taking something that you built from scratch and watch it blossom into something you can look upon with pride is what every entrepreneur who dives into business, hopes to accomplish one day. Profit margins may be small with dropshipping, but there is still potential to scale your business as far as it can go. Scaling, however, is going to present some rather unique, perhaps even interesting challenges along the way if you're up for it.

There are several factors that you need to consider when you're thinking about scaling your business, for example:

- Will you be able to handle the increasing demand for orders that come in and fulfill them in a timely manner?

- Are your order fulfillment methods right now being automated to keep up with demand?

- What about your order tracking? Is that automated yet?

- Can your customer service grow alongside your business so it always remains top-notch?

- What affiliate networks can you join to boost your profit margins?

- Will you be able to keep up the relationships that you've built with your supplier amid the increasing pressure of fulfilling larger order numbers in a timely fashion?

- Would your suppliers be willing to negotiate a cheaper price if you can promise to bring in more orders?

When it comes to advertising and marketing your product that you plan to sell through the dropshipping method, it is no different from marketing and promotional activities that you would employ for any type of business.

Marketing and advertising fundamentals are a must otherwise; how else would people know about you? In this chapter, we will cover the most important aspects of marketing your product specifically for the dropshipping method.

The great thing about using the dropshipping method is that you can concentrate all your efforts on marketing because the other aspects of the business are automated. But for the other aspects of the business to run, you first need to let people know you have this amazing product or service that they must buy and must use.

Let's be clear on a few of these basic elements which you must already have:

1. You must already have or already start working on a website
2. You need a logo
3. You need a blog
4. You need social media presence

Only once you've covered the fundamentals, we can actually look at optimizing your advertisement and marketing game. Here's what you can do:

Strategy #1- Building Trust

In this day and age, customer reviews carry the same weight as traditional word-of-mouth referrals. You read what other people have to say about a product and depending on their reviews; it influences you to buy or to ignore a certain product. Ratings, reviews and testimonials all add valuable weight to a customer's purchasing decision and it is an excellent way to build rapport and trust. Reviews help new visitors to your site see what other buyers have experienced and the more positive the reviews, the higher the potential of buying and completing a purchase.

You can encourage customer's review by adding a form in your website or sending them an email for a review. By encouraging reviews, you boost your conversion rate by 14 to 76 %.

Strategy #2- Creating an Amazing Offer

Visitors to your site may still be skeptical about buying. They could be worried about how a certain product may react or function for them. They could even be worried that they are that 1% of users who have bad experiences using your product or service. So how do you convert them into paying customers? Sales are your best bet. Doing a sale for new products or services at attractive prices allows potential customers the possibility of testing your product without paying full price. If they like it, they'll want to purchase from you again. Presenting the right product with the right deal will earn you higher converts.

Strategy #3- Preparing to Pivot

Dropshipping is a great business model for budding entrepreneurs since it is extremely easy to start up. Despite that, it is still a business and like any other business, you will experience obstacles and challenges along the way. When this happens, you need to find a way to overcome adversities and problems.

In your mission of running a profitable dropshipping business, be prepared to pivot at different intervals as your store grows. There may be a new trend that might come into the scene which you must add quickly to your store or there may be a product that you are forced to remove from your store because your customers don't like it. You may have invested in an ad that doesn't seem to be performing well.

Pivoting at these instances must be viewed as a requirement rather than a bad thing because only from our mistakes or problems do we learn how to make our business better.

Strategy #4- Choosing ePacket

ePacket shipping allows you to sort products and it is the fastest and most affordable shipping method for dropshippers. You will be guaranteed quick delivery to your customers without breaking the bank. Shipping costs for ePacket is usually under $5 and this allows for a decent profit when you sell products at market value. ePacket deliveries usually reach customers within a week of purchase and this not only makes for better customer service but it is also the best delivery method dropshippers can use.

Strategy #5- Importing the First 25 Items

When you start on your dropshipping store, the focus is important. Instead of importing 600 products in one day, you should concentrate your efforts into 25 items within the first few hours and ensure that you upload the right items and product descriptions to each of these items. Adding 600 items and its corresponding images and descriptions is not only time consuming but it is also exhausting and could decrease your productivity.

Always start with a smaller collection and you would be able to launch your business in a more focused way. From there on, you can add 10 products at a time to build on the collection you already have. You do not need 600 products to get your first sale. You just need one amazing product to land a good sale.

Strategy #6- Encouraging Upsell and Cross-sell Marketing

In a dropshipping business, you want to maximize your transactions in any possible way. Utilizing product upselling and cross-selling methods can jumpstart your transactional value. One of the ways of doing this is a 'Buy 1 Free 1' or 'Buy for a Friend' or even 'Frequently Bought Together' promo. Customers will be more inclined to purchase if a product comes in bundled with something else because there is more value in it.

Strategy #7 - Market on Social Media

Social media has become virtually impossible to avoid in today's tech-driven society. It's everywhere you go, in every business ad campaign you see. Businesses, both big and small, have come to terms with making social media a part of their marketing strategy and now that you plan to run your own dropshipping business, social media is going to become a part of your strategy to scale your business. Social media platforms boast billions of users worldwide who are actively on at least one of these platforms daily. That's a potential to reach billions of customers just by being present in that space alone. An opportunity to reach audiences far and wide is something you simply can't afford to pass up, not when it means the potential for more business. Social media must be leveraged on if you hope to scale your business moving forward.

Running Your Business

Did you think trying to maintain the discipline needed to survive in your 9 to 5 job was hard? Just wait until you start getting into running a business of your own. The commitment and investment needed in terms of time and money are going to be demanding, but if you love what you do, it'll be well worth it.

First things first, though, how much do you understand about the finances of this business you're about to undertake? Before you decide on investing your money into any kind of venture, it is important to understand some financial basics, specifically how much you'll be able to reasonably invest in your business and its future scaling efforts, your business cash flow and how to forecast your finances. The future of your business depends on the financial decisions that you make right from the start and every day after that. Give this some serious thought because the future of your business is riding on it. Seek assistance from a family member or friend, maybe even professionally or from a business mentor you may know of, if financials are not your strong point. Failing to get a good grasp of your finances is how many businesses ultimately end up failing miserably when they weren't supposed to.

Next, you would have to give some serious thought about your goals. What was the driving force that motivated you to begin this business in the first place? Is that reason sustainable in the long-term or based off a short-term impulse decision? How do you foresee this dropshipping business venture leading you one step closer towards your goal? Dropshipping may be low-risk and easy to start, but it is still a serious business. Serious business requires serious commitment if you hope to get things done and see your business going somewhere instead of just staying stagnant.

You need to commit. Commit to what you're doing wholeheartedly and completely. This is one something you can start on a whim one day for the fun of it and abandon it few weeks down the road when you find it is moving slower than you expected, or when you've lost interest and you've moved onto the next project you set your sights on. You may not be making massive profits right from the beginning, *but you will be making steady profits* if you continue working hard at it and not give up when the going gets tough. If you start this, you need to commit to seeing it all the way through, so your business has a fighting chance of survival as it competes against the thousands of other dropshipping websites out there.

You need to invest your time. Every second of our lives is precious and once a moment is gone, it's gone forever. We only have a limited amount of time to spend in this lifetime, so each moment has to count and it starts with a conscious choice of *what you want to do with your time* that will be most beneficial to you. A dropshipping business needs you to commit your time and energy to learn the ropes and understanding what your target market needs. This business is going to ask you to invest the time needed to be spent thinking about all the ways in which you can improve and grow your business and how to make best informed decisions that will keep your business a step ahead. You need to commit to the effort and time that is needed to keep the business running because this is going to be an ongoing thing for the next few years. Before you begin, you need to ask yourself if this is a venture you're willing to invest the hours for.

You need to invest some money. That's the way business works. To spend money you need to make some money and one way to do that is to invest in your dropshipping business *after you've done the proper research.* True, the sum that you're going to spend is considerably smaller than what you would have to pay if you were establishing a business the old-fashioned way, but the investment is still an investment nonetheless and should never be taken lightly. Money is a serious subject and you need to tread carefully by doing your due diligence before each business decision is executed. Ask yourself if the step you're taking is a worthy investment of your money and unless you're 100% certain about a move to make, it is best not to make any move at all. The wrong one can end up costing you more than you bargained for.

Choosing Your Dropshipping Business Structure

A legitimate business needs to have a legal structure to it. You may be running your dropshipping business online, but it is still a legal business that you're running. E-Commerce is just as much a legitimate business as the brick and mortar types and here are some business entity options that you could consider when establishing your own dropshipping venture:

- **Sole Proprietorship** - Planning to run your business solo? Then a sole proprietorship is the best choice to go with. The procedures involved are straightforward enough and it won't take too long for you to implement this structure once you've got all the necessary paperwork prepared. The requirements you need to fulfill are minimal and as long as you report your personal and business earnings for tax purposes, you're good to go. The only drawback with the sole proprietorship entity is that it offers no personal protection whatsoever, making you liable to bear the cost of any damages or legal issues that might come up. Your personal assets are going to be considered a part of your business structure. If your business is being sued, you're the one who's getting sued.

- **LLC (Limited Liability Company)** - The advantage of going with an LLC company is you don't have to worry about your personal assets being in jeopardy. They'll be protected because an LLC is going to be a separate legal entity and not tied to you personally. To set up this business structure, you'll be required to fulfill the necessary filing requirements and pay any fees incurred during the process.

- **C Corporations** - If properly established, this business structure offers you more protection in terms of liability compared to most other types of businesses. However, C Corporations tend to be a little more on the expensive side, on top of being liable for double taxation since any income earned from this structure is not passed onto the shareholders.

The type of business structure that you end up choosing for yourself is going to depend entirely on what your business requirements will be. Most entrepreneurs prefer either the sole proprietorship if they're going at it alone, or an LLC for the personal protection that it offers, especially for their finances.

Before starting any kind of business venture, you need to get your finances sorted out. It is never a good idea to blend both your personal and business financials together if you can help it. Keeping them separate makes it easier to keep track of your cash flow, especially for accounting purposes. The best advice would be to consider opening a separate bank account under the name of your registered business to track your spending. Options for bank accounts could include a business checking account, PayPal or even getting your own credit card, since credit cards are the preferred method of payment by many suppliers and customers alike.

The credit card should be kept separate and only for business expenses alone, not personal. These cards can be used to make the purchases you need from your supplier and if it's connected to your business account, some credit cards even offer great reward programs for businesses.

Dealing with Sales Tax and Local Licenses

Part of running a business is going to be getting involved in the tax aspect of it. Should your business fall into any of the following categories, you'll need to collect your sales taxes:

- If you happen to be living or running your business in a state where sales taxes are collected.
- If an order is made by a customer who lives in a state that implements sales tax.

Tax laws are beneficial for online merchants, particularly those who are new to running a dropshipping business.

Another thing that your business is going to need is a local license, which will require renewal on a regular basis. Business license requirements may be slightly different for those running a dropshipping business since you're most likely going to be running your business out of your own home. Be sure to check on the local laws and regulatory requirements before getting started.

Chapter 5: Handling Your Affairs

You're halfway through now working out the more subtle details and you'll soon be ready to have your dropshipping business up and running.

The next part of the set-up process to focus on, is the customer service aspect of it, which is also a very important area that must not be overlooked. Your customers are the lifeline of your business, without them, there wouldn't be any business to begin with. You need to sell your products to someone and when you depend on these customers for the survival of your business, you need to take care of them so they'll always come back to you.

How to Handle Customer Care

Competition may be tough in the dropshipping world, but one of the few ways to really stand out is through exceptional and absolutely remarkable customer service and support. Customers want to know that they matter and they should since they're giving you their money. They don't just want to see good quality products anymore, that's not going to cut it. They need to see that your store is responsive to their queries and makes an effort to clarify or resolve issues in the fastest way possible. They want good customer service.

Profits matter in any business medium, but not as much as great customer service does. In any business model, customer service is the only thing that matters. In a model as small as dropshipping where you need to maximize every avenue that you can to secure and sale and take home your profit, exceptional customer service is the life vest that is going to keep your business afloat. Going the extra mile with your customer service is not that difficult either, once you know which areas to focus on:

Handling Order Delays

Having your order delayed is something no customer ever wants to hear. You're not the one handling the stock, but you're the one who's going to take the heat from the customer when there's a delay in the orders. It's going to happen from time to time, where your supplier runs out of stock just when your customer has placed an order.

This is bound to happen once in a while and when it does, don't worry, there's a way to manage the situation and still keep your customers happy. Manage the situation well and you minimize the risk of losing the customers when they see that you care enough to try and find a workable solution that keeps everyone happy. When a delay in your shipment happens, the first thing you need to do is contact the supplier immediately to find out what happened and the reason behind the delay in getting the order processed. As soon as you've got your reason, the next immediate action is to contact your customers and be honest about what happened. Assure them that you're doing your best to speed up the process and get their order to them on time. Keep them updated every step of the way so they're never left out of the loop.

Handling Out of Stock Products

Keeping in frequent contact with your supplier is the only way to stay on top of your inventory and minimize the instances where customers place orders for out of stock products. This would be the ideal scenario, of course, but sometimes it's not always possible to prevent it entirely. Once in a while, a customer may order something that, as it turns out, is out of stock.

While it's best to prevent this situation entirely, that's not always the case and as a backup, you should have more than one supplier on hand who deals with the same products. That way, if one supplier is out of stock, you can turn to your back-up supplier and get them to ship out the order instead. Worst case scenario would be to email your customer directly and let them know, unfortunately, the product is out of stock and offer your sincere apologies and a few possible solutions that they could choose from. They might not be happy about the out of stock products, but at least you let them know rather than keep silent about it.

Every Little Bit Helps

Offering outstanding and unbeatable customer service is one of the best ways to stand out and set yourself apart from the competition, especially when you are selling the same products as every other merchant out there. Going the extra mile is always going to be worth the effort. Your customer service can be in the form of thank you cards included in the shipping packages. It could also be points that they have accumulated from multiple purchases which entitle them to a free gift or redeem a voucher on their next purchase. It can also be simple things like a speedy response to their issues or complaints. Whatever it is, the key is to make your customers feel valued and appreciated. Remember that without them, there wouldn't be a business for you to run.

A couple of other tips to provide excellent customer support and services include:

- Hiring a professional customer service executive if your budget permits. Having dedicated personnel specifically to respond to customer complaints in a speedy manner and keep communication channels open, will make your customer feel good, even if they are unhappy about the issues faced with your order.

- Respond to them in a timely fashion; don't wait for days or weeks before you reply. More importantly, never ignore their attempts to reach out to you at all cost.

- Provide a detailed FAQ section on your website which addresses the common concerns almost every customer might have, along with step-by-step answers to resolving those problems.

- Practice placing orders on your site as though you were a customer and view the ordering process through the eyes of a customer, rating your own experience on your website. Was your website easy to navigate? Were there problems making purchases? If you had a question, was it answered sufficiently in your FAQ section? If you have a dedicated customer support team, how quickly did they follow up with a reply to your query?

- Check on the items listed on your website frequently and make sure all stock numbers reflect an accurate picture of the items your supplier has on hand at the moment.

- Always try to stay at least one step ahead of your customers by putting yourself in their shoes and anticipating what questions, queries or concerns they might have regarding your products.

- Be as detail-oriented as possible and read your product descriptions with a critical eye. Do they provide enough information to your customers?

- Make it a point to personally thank the customer for leaving a positive review on your website. If they took the time to say something nice about you, then you can certainly make the time to thank them for it.

How to Deal with Frauds

Running a business online comes with its own set of risks different to that of physical businesses. One type of risk that both business mediums are in danger of experiencing though, is a fraud. Detecting fraud online is not always easy since these dangerous customer types often have a way of working around the system and coming up with newer, more creative ways to scam innocent internet users. Just when you thought you have them all figured out, they come along with a newer scam and if you're not paying attention and keeping your eyes and your instincts peeled for these fraudulent individuals, you might just become the next victim.

Dropshipping platforms like Shopify have evolved to accommodate instances like this, with own [fraud analysis](#) approach to detecting these sorts of problems. Say you received a large order from a client for example. As exciting as that is, you want to double check that this is a genuine order which has been placed and you can do that by emailing or contacting the customer directly and seek confirmation that this is the right order that they made. When your instincts kick in and start to warn you that something is not right, it's always best to listen.

When the billing address doesn't match up to the shipping address, stay on the alert, this could be a potential fraud order. Another example of what fraud orders may look like is when a customer sends a payment through to you via PayPal eChecks but cancels it once you've shipped out the order to them. It's best to wait until the payment is confirmed in your PayPal account before fulfilling the order, just in case something like this happens.

It is always best to proceed with caution when dealing with anything online, just to be on the safe side and protect yourself from fraud. Credit card fraud is particularly popular and it continues to be among the more common online scams since these tricksters are getting smarter and relying on more sophisticated measures of pulling off their frauds. It's not always easy to detect either, but paying close attention will let you spot the warning signs:

- Different names from the person who placed the order and the one who is receiving could be a red flag fraud trigger, but it could also be a customer sending a gift to another. Better check on the orders just to be safe.

- Watch out for differences in billing and shipping addresses. Different addresses might sometimes occur during the holiday or festive seasons when people shop online for gifts, but just to be safe it's always better to double check when you see two different shipping addresses.

- Stay alert if the email addresses look suspiciously like it could be a fraud. Email addresses which don't make sense are often a warning sign and the smart thing to do to protect yourself would be to remain vigilant.

- Cybercriminals have sometimes been known to spend extra on expedited shipping so merchants don't have enough time to figure out something might be amiss, like perhaps a stolen credit card being used to make those orders.
- When you receive an order, which is then immediately followed by a request to re-route the order, ask your information that clarifies this is a genuine order and not a fraud. A cybercriminal mastermind could be using this approach to bypass the usual security procedures which might flag their order as suspicious, so just be careful when you receive such requests since you never know who might be behind it.

Dealing with fraudulent orders can be a real hassle, not to mention unnecessarily time consuming and a waste of resources which could have been better spent on other aspects of your business. Keeping your eye out for those warning signs is not enough to protect you and your business entirely from the scammers who are always looking to make a quick buck off someone else's hard work and the best solution in this scenario to protect yourself from credit card fraud (or any kind of fraud for that matter) is to consider a more comprehensive form of fraud protection. This would usually be a combination of both manually monitoring and looking out for the signs and some automated solutions to detect signs of a fraud that will alert you when an order might not be legitimate.

Unfortunately, it is not going to be possible to completely protect your business from fraud altogether and this is just part of the risk that you need to be willing to undertake when you decide to run a business online. You may not be able to prevent it 100%, but you can employ the following measures to help minimize the risk of becoming a victim of online fraud:

- Require that customers' key in the CVV numbers (the last 3 numbers which appear at the back of every credit or debit card), this is one way of ensuring the person who is placing the order has a physical copy of the card in front of them.

- Use payment gateway services that come with address verification services or AVS, which is a security feature that ensures billing addresses provided are a match to the cardholder's zip code that the bank has on file in their records. If the details are not a match, the order will be rejected.

- Always remain vigilant with larger orders; these are the

ones where fraud is most likely to occur. Always screen larger orders and orders with different billing and shipping addresses.

How to Handle Product Returns

When business is doing really great and everything is running as it should, you're feeling buoyant, enjoying the thrill of running your own business for the first time (maybe). Suddenly, out of nowhere, you're hit by one of the few things no business owner ever wants to deal with. Product returns. Something that no business owner or customer ever wants to deal with. It's a hassle for you and it's a hassle for the customer and if you don't play your cards right, you're going to be left with a very angry customer and some potential reputation-damaging negative reviews. Handle returns well, though, and you'll be facing an entirely different scenario altogether.

Product returns are another norm when you're running a dropshipping business. There are bound to be one or two customers who are extremely picky about their products and if it doesn't live up to their expectations, they'll return it and request a refund. Among the common reasons for product return scenarios include inaccurate descriptions that painted a false picture of what the product was, problems with sizing, defective or faulty products and having the wrong items, delivered to them by mistake are among the many reasons why a customer might request a refund from your store. Whatever the reason may be, the bottom line is your customers are not happy and they want a refund.

Should you encounter this problem, here's what you need to do to handle it. First, establish strong and clear agreements on any potential logistical issues that you may encounter in your dropshipping business. Outline these in your contract and also have this on your website. Inform customers what to do if they have returned. Familiarize yourself with the return policy that your supplier has and outline this and establish standard operating procedures for returns, damaged items and so on. Your return policy must be in line with the one of your supplier. Be clear on what the shipping costs are as well between yourself and the supplier and what is the expected delivery date for your items between supplier and customer.

There's going to be two primary focus areas that need your attention when it comes to product returns. The first being your preparation in case a return happens and the second is what you're going to do once the returns do happen. What policies do you have in place to handle situations like this and are these policies taking into consideration your customers point of view? Have you taken preemptive measures to set clear expectations in place on your website when it comes to handling product returns and refunds? With over 67% of online customers making a point to check the returns policy of a company *before* making a purchase, expectations need to be set loud and clear right from the beginning so your customer can make a swift and easy decision about whether they want to make a purchase from your business or not. It's a good idea to have some kind of working standard agreement or procedure in place when dealing with return items to make the whole process easier for everyone in general. Customers may be put off by your store if they find it too difficult or complicated to deal with returns and that will cause them to take their business elsewhere. You, as the seller, need to make it a point to listen to the concerns or complaints that they raise, be empathetic and assure them that you're looking into this matter and aim to resolve it as soon as you can.

The following factors need to be considered when you're preparing your returns policy:

- Be sure to clearly list out any items which may be exempted from returns and the reasons why. For example, some items might not be eligible for returns because they're clearance items, or for hygiene purposes.

- Clarify the cost of your returns if they are not done for free.

- Be clear about whether your policy is to issue refunds or exchanges.

- Be specific about the countries which are eligible for returns and which are not.

- State clearly how long a customer has before they are no longer eligible for free returns, like a 30-day free return policy for example.

Handling product returns is no fun, but here's what you can do to make the process less stressful on all parties involved:

- **Keep Your Focus on Solutions Instead of Problems -** It's much easier to let the negatives and the complaints overshadow the good stuff, but to create a positive return experience for your customer so they'll come back again to your store, it is important that you actively choose to focus on the solutions instead of the problems at hand. Your customer is not going to care that it was your supplier who messed up, they're going to care that they didn't receive the item they were expecting to get and they want to be compensated for it. As the vendor, apologizing to your customer for the inconvenience it has caused shows them that you're willing to step up and take responsibility. Since actions speak louder than words ever will, it is going to be a lot more convincing for your customers that you actually care when they see you taking proactive measures to come up with workable solutions instead of trying to avoid blame or pinning the blame on someone else altogether.

- **Is A Return Necessary?** - That would depend on the product that you're dealing with. If an item is not worth getting the customer to ship it back to you (as is the case with most low-cost items), it might be best just to let it go and save them the hassle too of having to go out of their way just to return an item they were expecting to be satisfied within the first place. Weigh your pros and cons and decide if it would be better to just ship them a new one without having to deal with the hassle of returns. They'll be surprisingly grateful to be saved from all that extra work involved and they'll remember the great customer service that you provided them with.

- **Do It Yourself** - Let's say, though, that the returned item in question was on the expensive side, it might be best to get your customers to return the items directly to you instead of the supplier. For one thing, it allows you to see first-hand and determine if the quality of the product really was as bad as the customer claimed it was and for another, when you want something done right, sometimes you just have to do it yourself, as is the case with returns. Getting the customer to ship the items directly to you gives you the opportunity to get involved and sort it out for yourself, which may provide an overall better outcome and customer experience. You'll also get the opportunity to witness first-hand what your supplier's return policies are like, how long they take to fulfill those return orders and whether they're living up to the standards that they promised in the initial agreement.

- **Be Accountable** - This dropshipping business is yours, something that you chose to build and in doing so, you're solely responsible for the business in its entirety. If it's a success, you're responsible for it. If it's a failure, you're responsible for that too. When a customer requests a return, you must be responsible and accountable for it, even if it is not your fault entirely. Passing the blame and pointing the finger at your supplier instead is not going to resolve anything. Your customer is still going to be unhappy and you're going to come off as looking unprofessional if you're trying to pin the blame on someone else. Own up to the mistake and focus on trying to fix instead of blame.

- **Be Respectful and Patient** - There may be some customers who push your buttons with their unrealistic demands, but as an entrepreneur and business owner, it is your job to maintain professional and respectful composure at all times. Reacting poorly to a demanding customer is only going to reflect badly on your business and, in such a competitive environment, you can't afford any kind of negativity if you can help it. No matter how much a customer may try your patience, avoid being dismissive or rude towards both them and your supplier. Things happen beyond anyone's control every now and then, but losing your cool is never a good approach to solving any kind of problem. Being respectful and patient towards all parties involved however, gets the job done and improves your chances of trying to come up with an amicable solution that all parties involved will be happy with.

Should I Offer Product Returns and Why?

Ideally, no vendor would want to deal with return items or refunds if they could have it their way, but it still happens. It's too bad the order didn't pan out quite as you hoped, but what would be an even bigger shame is if the customer was put off ever making a purchase from your store again because of the bad experience they had shopping with you. If a customer is not happy with an item, they would rather return it and try to get their money back or replace it with something of similar value and when you take that option away from them, they'll be less inclined to want to do business with you.

So yes, you *must offer product returns* on your website because keeping your customers happy and satisfied is vital. A happy customer means a returning customer and a returning customer is a money-in-the-bank for you. It's going to be in your best interest to provide them with a customer service experience they have no complaints about and having a returns policy makes this a more viable option. As a dropshipping vendor, there's one other option available to you and that is offering your customers a refund, but they don't have to return the product to you. That's right, what you can alternatively do to minimize the hassle is ask your customer if they would prefer to be sent a new product *instead* of getting a refund and tell them that they can keep the product that they have right now without the need to return it.

Here's why that approach is a good idea. It makes your customers happy, since they don't usually expect this kind of service and depending on the size of your profit margins, if it's big enough you'll still be able to walk away at the end of the day with a positive revenue return too. This can still prove to be a great workable solution unless of course the item the customer has is either damaged or unusable.

What the Product Return Process Looks Like
For the first time dropshippers who might not be familiar with what the product return process might involve, here's what you can expect to encounter:

- **Step 1: The Return.** Your customer receives the order but then contacts you about making a return request. As the vendor, you would first need to determine the reason behind the returns request. Once you've determined it's a reasonable request, apologize and tell them you're sorry the product didn't quite live up to their expectations. Let them know that you're working on resolving the issue and will keep them updated every step of the way.

- **Step 2: The RMA.** Once your customer has confirmed they would like to proceed with the return request after Step 1 is accomplished, you would then need to get in touch with your supplier for an RMA number, which is a Return Merchandise Authorization number.

- **Step 3: The Approval.** The supplier should approve the return and then proceed to issue you with an RMA number for the order, you will then pass this RMA number along to the customer, together with a return address to send it to. If your customer needs to pay for shipping, remind them to get a tracking number for their order so they can keep tabs on it too.

- **Step 4: The Inspection -** If your customer is returning the product directly to you so you can handle the returns, inspect the item thoroughly and see if your customer's claims match up. In the case of damaged goods, be sure to take detailed pictures so you can send to the supplier for record purposes. If the customer is shipping it back directly to the supplier, keep tabs and communicate with the supplier to track the progress of this request.

- **Step 5: The Final Step -** By this stage, your customers should either be receiving a new item as a replacement or a refund depending on your returns policy and what the customer requested. Follow-up with your customer to confirm that the package has, in fact, arrived safely and they're perfectly happy with the new item that they received. If they requested a refund, follow-up anyway and check if they received the correct refund amount. Ask if there is anything else that you can do to assist them and let them know that they can contact you at any time if they have more questions or concerns.

The Product Return Process in Dropshipping
Picture 7

Other Considerations to Keep in Mind

Dealing with matters like refunds is another example of why it is so important to find a good supplier to work with from the beginning. You want a supplier who is professional and willing to accommodate refund requests patiently for the customers the way that you want to. Since you're not likely to be the one who handles the returns part as the vendor, you need to find a supplier who does accommodate returns and refunds as part of their standard operating procedure.

Before committing to any supplier, get to know their return and refund policy in greater detail and see if it lines up with the policy that you hope to offer as part of your dropshipping business. Be sure to outline the terms of the agreement clearly in your contract before signing any kind of documents with your supplier as a precaution to protect yourself against any possible liability issues.

Working with a supplier who is not willing to offer any kind of return or refund policy is a very risky move on your part. It's advisable to stay away from suppliers like this since your customers are not going to be very happy knowing that they can't return a product if they're not happy with it. No customer wants to be stuck with something they don't want and every business needs to offer the option of a return, even if it may be a hassle.

If you're concerned about the logistics of it all, it could be something to consider when you think about whether you want to work with a domestic or overseas supplier. Of course, handling overseas returns is a lot more complicated and sometimes expensive for the customer if they have to be the one who foots the bill, something they won't be too happy about. When you've been in business long enough, you're bound to deal with a refund or several and ignoring such requests is just not an option if you want to maintain the reputation of your business. Some customers might not be too happy dealing with a delay in returns either if they have to ship the products overseas back to the supplier. These are just some of the considerations to keep in mind when you choose which suppliers you would prefer to work with.

Returns will happen, even when you're working hard to make sure your business runs perfectly, therefore don't be too discouraged by it when you're hit with a refund or returns request. This is part and parcel of what it's like to run a business. Even retail establishments have to deal with product returns on a regular basis, so don't worry too much about it, it's not a negative reflection of your efforts in any way. Every business comes with its own challenges and drawbacks and in the e-commerce space, returns are normal. It's a drawback to be sure, but since it rarely happens (unless your store provides really terrible products and services), the benefits that you get from running your own business are still going to outweigh the drawbacks that you face.

Since refunds are something you need to consider, it's best to be very careful with the profits that you make from your business. Avoid spending it all at once, especially in the early stages of your business. You might need to hold onto those profits for a while just to cover any instances of a product return or refund. It may not happen all that often, but at least when it does, you're well and truly prepared to deal with it.

Chapter 6: Success Is Almost Yours

We're nearly close now to finalizing your dropshipping business set-up. Now that you've covered some of the important basics, it's time to look at how to successfully fulfill the orders that come in from your customers. As a business owner, you want all your customers to walk away feeling happy and satisfied like they had the best shopping experience on your website from the order process to the customer service follow up. It has to be so good that they can't wait to come back and do it again. That's the kind of experience you want to aim for. To do that, you need to perfect the order fulfillment process.

Order Fulfillment - What Is It Anyway?

This side of the business basically involves the steps that get taken by you and your supplier to get the product shipped out to your customer. The steps that take place from the time they place their order with you and everything that happens in between until the order arrives safely on their doorstep. Once you've established your niche and locked down the suppliers that you want to work with, it becomes easier to fulfill the orders that come in so your business can build a sustainable momentum that keeps it going. Hopefully with an increase in profits over time, if you play your cards right.

Dropshipping is a *service* which you are providing and the order fulfillment process is part of that overall service. The very critical role that you are playing in the dropshipping scenario is ensuring that the products which get ordered through your website are shipped out in a timely manner. That your customer is getting what they want. Seeing your first few orders come in after your website has been successfully launched and your business finally going live online is exciting, but what you do *after* those orders come in is what really matters most. This is when you determine if your business is going to leave a positive impression in the eyes of your customer or leave them with a sour taste in their mouth and the determination never to buy from your store ever again.

What happens next is crucial to building a positive reputation for your business and when the competition is as high as it is in dropshipping, the image is going to be everything. Before getting to those steps and what you need to do is start cultivating that positive shopping experience through your order fulfillment, here's a brief overview of what the order fulfillment process is going to look like:

- Customers' places order on websites created for your

website.

- Payment is made and confirmed. The customer then gets an email notifying them that their order has been successfully placed.

- You send the details of this order to the supplier.

- Once the supplier has confirmed that the items are in stock, the wholesaler will box and ship the items directly to the customer.

- Once the shipment has been finalized and sent out successfully, the supplier will then email you a copy of the invoice with the tracking number and all the relevant details. Depending on the supplier that you're using and stock availability, some suppliers will ship out products within a few hours of receiving the order, which will give you the advantage of advertising same-day shipping or 24-hour shopping.

- Once you have received the shipment tracking number from your supplier, you will need to send these details to the customer. You can do this either directly via email, or automated through the built-in feature on your e-commerce site's interface.

- Once the product has been shipped out, the payment received and collected and the customer has been notified, only *then* is your order considered fulfilled and complete.

Your profit from this order fulfillment will depend on the difference which was charged to your customer and how much you had to pay your supplier. You will be the contact point for the customer if they need to reach out to you for anything. If they receive the wrong order, you will be their point of contact, not the supplier. Your role is to merely coordinate with your supplier to ensure all the order details get fulfilled the way that they should.

To your customer, the supplier does not exist in this sales scenario. It is just a transaction between you and them. Therefore, in the order fulfillment process, it is going to be entirely your responsibility to ensure the success of the sale. You will be doing everything from advertising on your website, marketing your products, providing the necessary customer service needed and more.

Creating a Positive Sales Experience for Your Customer

Whether your customer walks away happy and satisfied with their overall sales experience with your store is going to be entirely up to you and what you do during the order fulfillment processes. Delays and hiccups along the way with orders getting fulfilled can sometimes set you back and put the customer off, so you want to do everything that you can to make sure the transaction flows as smoothly as possible.

To create a positive sales experience for your customer, you need to:

- **Check Your Settings** - Have you set up your order process to be fully automated? If you haven't, you should. Check your settings and activate the options which allow you to mark orders as being "processed" and "shipped". You can rely on the manual way of doing things, but that's a bit risky since you might forget to do it if you've got other tasks in your business that need attending to.

- **Not Procrastinate** - As soon as the order comes in, get to work. Don't wait and don't procrastinate. The faster you get things done, the faster your order gets shipped out and if you want to keep your customers happy, there's not a minute to lose. Ideally, you want to have your orders shipped out within 24-hours after the customer has placed an order and any delays on your part could prove to be costly affairs.

- **Confirm the Shipping Details** - Always check the shipping information listed on your package before your orders get sent out. It simply won't do to have the items shipped to the wrong person, this would only cause further delays, complications and most likely you're going to have to spend out of your own pocket replacing the order for your customer. Check that the names are written and spelled correctly, check that the addresses are written correctly and check that the contact information has been written out correctly. Check, double check and then check again just to be safe.

- **Use Message Templates** - Information is everything to your customer and when they've had to pay for something, you can be sure they want to know what's going on. Consider using message templates that keep your customer updated about the status of their order from the time they make the payment and all the way up to when their items are out for delivery. They'll appreciate being kept in the loop and it helps if they don't have to keep emailing you or following up about what's happening with their orders.

- **Keep Things Simple** - Your main goal is to create profits, right? That should be your focus. Do not get carried away by flashy graphics and so call 'must-haves' for your website or even long content that apparently 'speaks' to your audience. Make it as easy as possible for the customers to purchase your products. The idea is to get them to your site, browse for what they want, click on the product, read a short description and click on Add to Cart > Proceed to Checkout. That's it.

- **Tracking Your Traffic** - Always keep your eyes on the traffic coming into your website and who is placing orders for your products. You might be surprised to find that every now and then you might receive an order that comes from a customer outside your target demographic. Perhaps the target audience is changing or expanding and if you're not on top of things, you might miss out on the opportunity to broaden your reach.

- **Be Organized** - A merchant who is organized keeps their customers happy because this merchant knows exactly what is happening every step of the way. An organized merchant keeps their order process just as smooth flowing and as organized as they are and that inspires confidence in customers.

After your orders have been placed, you need to mark your orders as either "fulfilled" or "completed". And that is how you successfully complete the order fulfillment process in your dropshipping business.

What to Do When You Can't Fulfil Your Orders

Luck may not always be on your side sometimes and despite doing everything that you can to make sure it all goes well, you may find yourself on an occasion or two where you're simply unable to fulfill the orders as you promised. Moments like these are sometimes beyond your control and that's okay. Understandably, it's distressing when you feel like you're failing to deliver on a promise to your customer and you're worried and stressed over whether this is going to negatively impact your business. You don't want to lose your customer forever and you don't have to, not if you handle the situation correctly.

If you find yourself in a position where you're unable to fulfill an order, you need to address the problem as soon as you become aware of the situation. Don't wait a day or two before you let the customer know, let them know immediately and let them know what's going to happen from there. A simple *"Dear customer, we regret to inform you that we're unable to fulfill your order at this time. We sincerely apologize for any inconvenience this may have caused and we will be issuing you with a full refund"* is an example of a professional yet courteous correspondence that lets your customer know what is happening. Since you're acting in a professional capacity, you want to avoid adding too much of a personal touch into the mix.

The customer may have some questions about the reason for the delay. Answer them patiently and professionally, being mindful that you want to appease the customer and keep them happy since the inconvenience is coming from your side.

Tips for Success

Like every other entrepreneur who first began their journey with hopes and dreams of achieving business success, you want to do everything you can to give your business its best chance of success.

Let's look at some of the following tips for success that you can employ to boost the success of your dropshipping business before we move onto the mistakes you need to avoid:

- **SEO Matters -** This should be an integral part of your

marketing strategies. Yes, there is going to be marketing involved, even with a business model like dropshipping. Despite the many claims online, SEO is not dead and as long as keywords are still used to search for anything and everything on the internet. SEO must be incorporated not only on your website but also on your social media which is from content, titles, tags, image tags, descriptions to increase its chances of getting picked up by search engines.

- **Don't Underprice Your Products** - A business needs to make a profit, even if it's not a lot. But profits still need to be made and if you underprice your products too much, you're going to end up on the losing end and find yourself struggling to maintain your business. It's tempting to keep your prices low to match what your competitor is doing, but if it's not feasible to sustaining your business, it's not a good idea. It's best to offer quality products at a fair price, so even if your prices might be a little higher from your competitors, if the quality is significantly better your customers won't mind paying that little bit extra for something that lasts longer.

- **Think Like Your Customer** - You're going to have to think like a customer and put yourself in their shoes. If you were to go to a website where you would like to make a purchase, what do you expect to see? What sort of buying process is going to make you feel happy and satisfied with making a purchase? What are the features that you personally like from some of the websites that you have purchased from in the past? Give the customers what they want and they will be more likely to keep returning for more.

- **Provide A Contact Number** - If you can list a contact number on your store, do it so your customers can reach you if they desperately need to. They might not, but they will like knowing that they have that option to do so should they need it. It's one way of building trust and transparency with your customers, if they know that there's a way for them to reach you directly, they'll feel a lot more confident making a purchase from you as opposed to someone they have no way of getting in touch with.

- **Learn to Love Reviews** - There's that brief moment of worry when you wonder if you're going to be hit with a bad product review that could put a damper on sales, but if your service is good, you don't have to worry too much about it. Don't be afraid of product reviews, because this is the weapon that you need to encourage other users who have not purchased from your website before to *want to* *buy from you.* Honest product reviews help to convince new customers that they are making the right choice in choosing to purchase form your platform instead of your competitors.

- **Using Unique Photos** - A lot of dropshippers are going to be using the same supplier that you might be, which means the photos and images of the products which are going to be displayed on their websites are going to be similar stock images. Building a good relationship with your supplier is going to come in handy here. Ask your suppliers if they could provide you with some unique pictures of the product so your website is going to stand out against your competitor's. When your customer comes across something that looks different, they're going to be intrigued and linger on your website long enough to want to make a purchase hopefully.

- **Give Your Customers Options for Payment** - Customers love knowing they have options. The more options you give them, the happier they will feel making a purchase from your store because they have the option of choosing what they feel more comfortable with. PayPal, Apple Pay, Amazon Payments, Shopify Payments, Stripe Atlas, Visa, MasterCard and more, spoil your customers with choices and you'll be their first choice the next time they need to buy something.

- **Mixing It Up -** There are many ways to reach your customers depending on who they are and what they do. For most drop shipping marketing methods, social media marketing and email marketing is the way to go. But you should not rely on it entirely. On and off, it is also good to meet with your customers and see who they are. Give product giveaways, hold online workshops or seminars, have an online meet-and-greet, feature your customers using your product.

- **Product Strategy Communication -** Strong product descriptions ensure higher success rates of purchasing. This information is critical to your customer- they want to know what they are buying and the better you describe your product, the faster it would be for your customers to make a purchasing decision. Avoid long and vague descriptions and also do not put on duplicate content, because this will be penalized by the search engines.

Dropshipping Mistakes to Avoid

Protect your business even more by staying away from the common dropshipping mistakes that become the pitfall for many new entrepreneurs who are doing this, especially for the first time. Even the more experienced vendors are guilty of making these mistakes when they get too comfortable with the process and overlook a lot of the little details which are crucial to the survival of the business. Just because this business model is easy, doesn't mean that there's no room for mistakes to be made. There's *always* room for mistakes when you become too complacent and start taking a lot of things for granted.

If you want to succeed, you need to maximize your chances for success and minimize your chances of mistakes. This is the only formula you need to remember, the only one that works. Great success efforts, fewer mistakes and slip-ups. Whether you're new to this space or you've been dropshipping for a while now and you're looking to take your business a step further, if you're guilty of any of the following mistakes, it's time to put a stop to them:

- **Relying Entirely on Your Suppliers** - Relying 100% on your suppliers can be an invitation for plenty of problems ahead. Having one supplier alone, for example, can mean that they may raise prices for you or if they go out of business, or the items run out which means you may also go out of business. What would you do then? Having a backup supplier is what you should do. Working with one supplier alone is never a good idea, you always need to have backups. Have a Plan B for your Plan A and also have a Plan C for when Plan A and B don't work. When doing business in dropshipping, always have a written contract with your suppliers to ensure that both parties know what they need to do to keep their end of the bargain.

- **Fretting Too Much About Shipping Costs** - Yes, the cost of shipping can be a pain, but worrying never achieved anything productive. Your priorities need to be strategically aligned to increase sales and depending on where your orders come from, your shipping costs will be in a different range. So in the spirit of increasing your profits, a good thing to start with is setting a flat shipping rate that will reduce this worry for you. It is straightforward and easy for your customers and it will be easier for you.

- **Selling Goods Which Are Copyrighted or Trademark -** The last thing you want to do, is invite into your business potential legal problems. The situation is simple enough. You *cannot* under any circumstance sell goods which are trademarked or copyrighted unless you have the legal rights and permission to do so. You need a license to sell these and if you don't have one, don't sell them. It's really as simple as that. It's not worth the legal hassle of resolving these problems and it could end up costing you quite a fair amount, depending on the severity of the situation.

- **Starting This Business Because You Think It's Easy Money** - It's not. It's an easy business to start, but it's not easy money. As we already know, drop shipping does provide a good level of convenience that does make your job a simpler one. Despite that, you need to be aware of the competition ahead of you and how important it is to market your product. This needs research as well as a unique approach that makes your product stand out among the masses. Don't expect money to roll in without putting in the work needed and time as well to see your product and your site lift out.

- **Being Too Optimistic with Your Shipping Estimates** - If you're going to post on your website that you deliver the next day, you better believe that's what your customers will be expecting. If their package has not arrived on their doorstep by the next day, they're not going to be happy. As much as you want to entice your customers to purchase from you with the promise of delivering their items as soon as possible, you need to be realistic about the shipping times. Especially if your products are coming in from suppliers overseas. A supplier won't be able to give a guarantee about how long a shipment is going to take either since anything can happen to the package when it's en route. Delays happen, items get held up at customs and posting a delivery time frame of 2 days is not feasible if you can't manage it.

- **Difficult to Find Information** - Ease and simplicity are the two keywords you need to keep in mind when you think of your customer. Keeping your customers informed about the product they are buying, the way they make payments, the information they are keying into your site as well as how long they will need to wait till their items arrived are all the things you need to put in "Black and white". Not only will this help you troubleshoot problems but your customers will be happy with the information they can access.

- **Having Different Shipping Fees** - Customers are not going to be happy if they have to fork out extra money for certain items on your website. If they're buying several different products from you, they're going to expect the same shipping costs (maybe even free shipping) for one simple reason. They buying from the same website. There's an expectation that the shipping is going to be standard across the board no matter what item they buy since it's coming from one website, so having different shipping fees is never a good idea.

- **A Lack of Branding** - For the customers who are brand conscious, not having a prominent brand name or label to identify with is something they see as a problem. The one major drawback of dropshipping is that it can be hard to ensure that your brand is prominent to your customers not only in the look and feel but also the entire customer experience. You don't want your customers to forget you and you need to work extra hard to insert your brand as much as possible in every corner you can. One of the best things you can do is to ensure you develop a good working relationship with your supplier and get them to insert custom packaging for you to remind them of your business and show them you care about their experience at the same time.

- **Policies Which Are Too Vague or Generic** - This one works along the same lines as having product descriptions which are too vague, generic and severely lacking in important information. You need to have a policy that is going to fit the image and level of service you want your business to provide. Avoid the temptation to just copy and paste policies directly word for word from other websites, since their policies might not be in line with your standard operating procedure. It's okay to use some of the information, but you need to rewrite and reword the content to reflect the kind of service you intend to provide with your business.

- **Poor Handling of Lost or Damaged Items** - The minute a customer experiences problems with their order, their frustrations are immediately directed at you. When this happens, you need to be prepared to offer your customers an easy and quick solution. Be sure that you create a process for managing and handling problematic orders so you can keep your customers happy.

- **Poor Handling of Order Cancellations** - Your online customers change their minds faster than the ones who shop at regular stores. This is bound to happen and for this, you need a backup plan as well. You want to ensure that your customer is efficiently and accurately refunded. Some vendors will immediately go ahead and make the order and you'll end up with a negative review on your site. To avoid this, speak to your vendor first before confirming things with your customer. While your customers wait for confirmation, let them know you have received their request and are working on making the necessary refunds or changes.

- **Complications with Return Items** - Setting up a

system for returns will be beneficial not only for your sanity but also to lessen the time your customers need to wait for a result. Organized and systematic approaches to problems not only keep your customers happy but it also shows you are professional. All it takes is one bad experience with your store to turn your customers away and that's not the only thing you need to worry about. Customers talk and word of mouth spreads. If they're unhappy enough with your service, they'll be telling everyone that they know not to make purchases from your store and that puts your business in danger of losing customers fast.

- **Not Taking Holidays into Account** - Holidays can cause major delays in shipping and delivery and whenever there's a holiday coming up, you should be posting these updates about possible delays in shipment so your customer is fully aware when they place their order. That way, they can't come back to you and complain about a late delivery in their order because you've already done your part by keeping them informed. Choosing to proceed with the order despite the delay notifications will be their choice.

- **Not Having a Strong Enough Relationship with Your Suppliers** - Without a good working relationship, there's going to be a lot of problems down the road. This works the same in any kind of professional or working relationship, if there isn't a good working dynamic, it makes it harder to get the job done well. Find a supplier that you're completely comfortable with, someone that is easy to get along with, accommodating and willing to compromise and negotiate until you can come to an agreement that you're both happy about. Being able to communicate effectively with them makes it easier for you to stay on top of all the important information that you need to know about to keep your business operations running smoothly. This relationship is important and you need to bear in mind that you're not the only vendor that they're working with. If the supplier doesn't like this relationship or think it's not beneficial enough, they can terminate their ties with you at any time, too. You'll be left scrambling trying to find a replacement supplier and, meanwhile, you're unable to fulfill any orders in the process.

- **Not Checking Your Shipping Logistics Before Deciding Which Countries You Can Ship To -** Assuming that your business is going to be able to handle global shipping is a big mistake. Yes, there are many businesses these days that are going global, but only if they can afford to. You need to have the available resources to be able to pull this off for an affordable price, some countries can be pretty pricey to ship to if you're not careful. Always check on the shipping costs and how much time it would take to deliver items to certain countries before immediately listing that your store can ship globally without so much as a second thought. As a beginner to this space, your best bet would be to focus on shipping domestically and perhaps start with one or two overseas countries and see how things go from there. Some countries may take longer to ship than others, not to mention the customs issues that you need to deal with which might cause even more delays or make the shipping costs too expensive overall. Remember that your profit margins are small with dropshipping and you don't want to be spending too much on your shipping costs. You don't want to put too high a shipping fee on your products either, since your customers are going to be put off by that too.

Bonus Tips to Keep a Good Relationship Going with Your Supplier

It's easy to get along with your supplier when you make an effort to cultivate and foster that kind of relationship. Keeping things on good terms with the supplier is not difficult and the following measures are enough to start building the foundation of a long-term working relationship:

- Always treat them with respect and act professionally at all times, even when you're having a disagreement with them.

- Pay them on time and maintain a good payment history with your supplier.

- Make an effort to work together instead of immediately pointing fingers or putting the blame entirely on the supplier. Sometimes it isn't their fault and it's best to give them the benefit of the doubt. Playing the blame game never helped to resolve anything, so try to find a working solution instead is a much more productive approach and your supplier will appreciate your effort.

- If they're domestic-based, try to arrange to meet them in person every month or so. It helps to be able to put a face to the name you're working with and people always make a much better impression in person than they do online. You'd be surprised at just how well the personal touch element still works in today's digital age.

Conclusion

Thank for making it through to the end of this book, let's hope it was informative and able to provide you with all of the tools you need to achieve your goals whatever they may be.

Now that you've got all the power-packed information that you need to start, build and run your store, it's up to you to keep that store running by avoiding the common mistakes that ordinarily get made. More importantly, you've now discovered everything that you need to know about sourcing the right suppliers for your business. Like with any business model, getting started on the right foot is going to be the essential driving force of your success. The dropshipping industry is a competitive one, but now you've got all the techniques that you need to set yourself apart from the rest of your competitors.

For the entrepreneur who has always wanted to have a business of their own, but has always been afraid of the risks involved and the possibility of losing it all should the business fold, dropshipping offers the perfect solution. The simple, inexpensive retail model is ideal for even an entrepreneur with no experience to start learning the ropes and even if you fail don't worry about it. Since the costs involved in the start-up is minimal, you won't find yourself knee-deep in debt and you'll be able to use that experience as a learning curve.

You've already got everything that you need to get started, all that's left is to commit the necessary time, effort and resources needed to get your business off the ground.

Finally, if you found this book useful in any way, a review on Amazon is always appreciated!

By the same Author:

Printed in Great Britain
by Amazon